VENEZUELA

# VENEZUELA

Gabriel Gazsó

Photography and Text:
Fotos und Text: GABRIEL GAZSÓ

Presentation:
Vorwort: GUILLERMO MORON

English translation: JUAN RIVERO CHARLSTON
Deutsche Übersetzung: HANS REIMELT

Colour separation:
Farbseparation: MONTANA GRAFICA

Printing:
Druck: EDITORIAL ARTE, C.A., CARACAS

ISBN: 980-300-685-1

# CONTENTS

# INHALT

# THE PURPOSE OF THIS BOOK

Three important attainments in a productive life are considered to be: having a child, planting a tree and writing a book. Nevertheless, the gratest personal fulfillment is believed to be an artistic expression, and this is what I have tried to achieve in this book.

When the optical synthesis of a country is involved, as is the case here, the judgement affects the visual conceptualization of the country and consequently the foundations of the patriotic values necesary for its existence as a nation. This was also my intention.

This judgement is linked to the basic national values of the country whose portrait I am presenting, inasmuch, of course, as I am able to perceive them.

Venezuela is equally Caribbean, Amazonic, and Andean. Geologically, it comprises the primary through the quaternary ages. Thence, nature has greatly favored it. It spans seven dimensions: coast, sea and islands, rivers, jungles, plateaus, plains, and mountains.

I have attempted to show this country, with its beaches, sand, and palms, where the blue color blends with the turquoise. It has been my intention to bring the ancient mesas, the tepuyes, within a hand's reach, and to spread out throughout the Gran Sabana or great plains. I have tried to convey the feeling of the Orinoco river and its jungles. I have traveled in deserts and witnessed the struggle for existence. I have flown over the plains, the Llanos, where one infinite horizon is followed by another. I have journeyed throughout the Andes, where a harsh existence prevails, and where green fields are joined to blue skies. I have seen cities from the air and from the ground; I have observed the people, the clouds, the trees, the forests and the mountains. I have tried to depict Venezuela with a lens, the way I see and like it. In the process, I have imposed my own abstractions, my own simplifications, my own order, and my own hierarchy. I have kept the things that please me, those which I consider worthy of being copied and preserved, those which are inspiring, satisfying, and elevating.

My contribution was to try to exalt beauty, to retain things in their best form and, perhaps, in their best moment. I wanted to capture important but fleeting events, to emphasize permanent and lasting values. Thus, I have tried to capture aesthetics, that creative energy which embodies proportion, the absence of the superfluous and of the irrational, the lack of harshness and uselessness, and the absence of force as a substitute for reason.

And with this purpose, dear reader, I leave you with these images. Up to now they have been mine: I hope they will be yours from now on.

Gabriel Gazsó.

## WITNESSES OF THE FUTURE

The 916,455 square kilometers of this land have borne the name of Venezuela since 1501. The Spanish cartographer, Juan de La Cosa, used this denomination in the first map of America, and thus placed it on the imago mundi, the great universal map. The name of the country is confirmed by its birth certificate, the Real Cedula of 1528, the legal instrument which created the Province of Venezuela. Its territory was demarcated on the east by the cape of La Vela, on the west by Cumana, and to the south by the waters of the Orinoco river's left bank. With the addition of the Llanos or plains of Casanare and the entire Guajira peninsula, Venezuela became a Governance and Captain-Generalcy, an important component of the parent state, Spain.

Around the Venezuelan Center, other Governances and Captain-Generalcies were created by the Spanish rule: Margarita, in 1525; Cumana, 1568; Trinidad, 1591; Guayana, 1568; and the complex Province of La Grita-Merida-Maracaibo, which evolved from 1575 to 1678, when it finally became the Governance of Maracaibo. These entities were then equal to Venezuela both in political importance and in civilizing influence, a reflection of the Spanish culture and political influence.

Over three centuries, the original Spanish culture gradually evolved into its current form, taking on its characteristically Venezuelan hues. During the 18th century, the original province of 1528 consolidated itself. Not only because its people became "criollos", as we call ourselves, and because of crossbreeding, culturization, and civilization, but because new territory was acquired. Surrounding territories were adjoined to the Province with strong legal links: the Intendencia del Ejercito y Real Hacienda of 1776, the Captain-Generalcy of 1777, the Royal Audience (court) of Caracas 1786, and the Royal Consulate of 1792. These legal instruments were aimed at the unification of the territory under a single name, Venezuela.

Thanks to this process, the constitution of 1811 could establish a single republic; and the present one, under which we are governed, can affirm (article 7) that "the national territory is that which corresponded to the Captain-Generalcy of Venezuela before the transformation initiated in 1810, with the modifications resulting of valid treaties duly made by the republic". Indeed, the territory in 1810 covered 1,116,461 kilometers. The republic has witnessed a considerable loss. But the land is still ample, the home of today's Venezuelans, who inherit five hundred years of unbroken tradition.

The face of man reflects the face of the earth. Venezuela was home to many indian cultures. Many languages have been spoken here, since at least 15,000 years B.C. The Barrancas culture on the banks of the Orinoco, identified by anthropologist Manuel Sanoja Obediente, is only one of many. The works of Miguel Acosta Saignes and many published and ongoing researches in archaeology, linguistics and ethnology, all let us feel the presence of "homo venezuelanensis" long, long, before the current civilizing process began in 1501 with the founding of Santa Cruz on the Gulf of Venezuela, on the bay of Castilletes.

The old races are still represented, although most of them have been swept away by the torrent of our criollo culture. There remain some eighteen cultures in their native ecologies. Although the official numbers do not correspond to those of the anthropologists, there are somewhere between 70,000 and 350,000 indigenous natives in the country, a minoritary (0.9%) in the 1981 official population of 14,570,085. In contrast, the population of foreign extraction sums up to as much as 10%.

But the indigenous inhabitants still live on in the daily life of Venezuela through the interbreeding process, which was well established by the 17th century. Blacks also participated in the process, due to the enormous influx of African slaves. The Venezuelan people descend from these mixtures, with the Spanish culture predominating and giving us the Castilian language.

The Venezuelan people of the 1700s were unified socially and culturally, as well as politically. Sociology underscores the presence of the mestizo or racially mixed person, then called "pardo". Around the year 1800, Venezuela had about a million inhabitants, of which 800,000 were already criollo, impossible to differentiate by caste, color, or social behavior; the rest —blacks, indians, whites— were in the process of assimilation. This process was completed by the 19th century, when the population integrated itself with the country, became part of the land, or, in short, became Venezuelanized.

Venezuela in the deepest sense, the real Venezuelan, is an ancient, sunburnt man, almost five hundred years old, weather-beaten by history. This majority lives on —in towns, in hamlets, in cities founded in the 1600s— unified by the language, by idiosyncracies, by religion, by habits, usages, and customs. New alliances, forged mainly with Spaniards, Italians, Portuguese, and other Latin Americans, have fortified the original mixtures. The culture, five centuries of it, is traditional, some of it deriving from the so-called western and christian civilizations, but historically in the line of the greco-latin culture, colored by exchanges with aboriginal and some African cultures. Identity is found in the Spanish language, made official by the Constitution and made legitimate through heredity.

Contemporary history in Venezuela began in 1936. In the fifty years elapsed since then, Venezuela has consolidated itself and developed. It has confirmed its heritage, its racial mixture process, has made itself aware of its own presence and its own permanence. It has developed physically and spiritually along its own historical path.

In 1936 the country opened up to modern currents of expression and modern social ways. Modernization did not take place during the 19th century as would have been desirable, but during our own times. Politically, democracy won the battle over dictatorships. First, a liberal democracy with Eleazar Lopez

Contreras (1936-1941) and Isaias Medina Angarita (1941-1945); then an unbroken representative democracy which has prevailed since 1958. The economy underwent a drastic change, moving from an agricultural basis to one founded on the exportation of petroleum. Radical social changes have also taken place in the last fifty years. A rural population has become urbanized; public health measures have reduced infant mortality and raised life expectancy; illiteracy has dropped from 90% in 1936 to 12% in 1986; state-directed public education has become extensive to the point where 98.5% of the population between ages 7 and 13 is in school; two Universities have been increased to 97 institutes of higher learning. Progress makes itself visible in the constructions: colonial houses give way to modern skyscrapers in Caracas, Maracaibo, Valencia, and San Cristobal; each small city is undertaking the wearying task of modernization.

Of course, modernization is not just a material process, dealing with building roads, dams, and industrial plants, but is mainly a cultural task. Schools, universities, workshops, science, technology... all these underlie the capacity to modernize. The solidification of democracy, the transformation of the State, the possibility of dealing with our external debt, finding an economy to serve us now and in the future, all these depend on the cultural capacity of our people. The history of the next hundred years will tell us if Venezuela, in fact, was able to modernize. But meanwhile, this book of images is a witness of how the land and its inhabitants are ready to face the future.

Guillermo Morón.

# THE REGIONS OF VENEZUELA

# THE EAST

It was the year 1498, and the third day of August. It was also the third voyage to the West Indies under the command of Admiral Christopher Columbus. He was on board his favorite ship, the Niña, once called the Santa Clara, 36 meters in length, 11 meters in breadth. Square sails, decorated with red crosses, were set on three masts, 22, 18, and 11 meters high respectively.

The Admiral, who had sailed from Trinidad, was bound for the muddy waters of the Dragon's Mouth and anchored at what he called the Isle of Grace. He had arrived at Macuro, in the peninsula of Macarapana, today called Paria. At that time, this peninsula was thought to be an island.

However, it was on a real island called Cubagua, that Spain, in the year 1500, began the transplant of its social and political structures with the founding of Nueva Cadiz. A city of square blocks, complete with city hall, church, royal treasury, shops, and dwellings was laid out; it received its city charter in 1523.

The first municipal ordinance was approved by Doña Juana, queen of Spain, in Valladolid in 1538. Its dispositions would be hailed by any conservationist today:

> "...no one may dig holes, either on the beach or on the streets of the city, for construction purposes, without a license... garbage may not be dumped on beaches or streets... ships may not sail without clearance, except those to Margarita... sellers who do not pay their city taxes will suffer the confiscation of their goods...", to quote just a few.

Nueva Cadiz was erected on the island of Cubagua. Lacking water, vegetation, and animals, its only renewable natural resources were pearls, and this resource was not, in fact, renewed. As its economy dwindled, so did the population. In 1543, the city was finally destroyed by a tempest.

At this time, the Spanish conquistador had occupied the continent for half a century. The upshot had been one fort constructed on the mouth of the Neveri river, to guarantee the water supply to Cubagua; sundry expeditions to the Orinoco and Meta rivers; and the catechization, enslavement, or annihilation of the natives according to the ideology, whim, or mandate of the prevailing government.

After these beginnings, Oriente, or Eastern Venezuela, has passed through several periods: discovery was followed by conquest, and then in turn, by colonization, independence, civil wars, an agricultural economy and the petroleum period. Today, a new epoch seems to be emerging: the tourist age; the region is perhaps uniquely qualified in this respect.

Territorially, Oriente comprises the states of Anzoategui, Sucre, Nueva Esparta, and Monagas. All have coastlines except Monagas, and Nueva Esparta is insular (its islands are Margarita, Coche, and Cubagua). Economically, the region depends on oil, agriculture, fishery, and industries, among them cement.

Agriculturally, half of Venezuela's cacao (cocoa bean) is provided by this part of the country, as well as 14% of the nation's coffee crop.

Four National Parks have been established in this region: La Restinga, Mochima, the Guacharo, and the Paria Peninsula. This creation of "untouchable zones" follows the precedent of Simon Bolivar, an early conservationist, who in 1825 signed in Chuquisaca, Bolivia, a decree regulating the "...creation, prosperity, and destiny of forests...".

Thus, in 1978 the National Park of Paria is established by presidential decree. The park stretches west to east from Cabo (cape) Tres Puntas to Punta Peñas, an extension of 37,500 hectares. On the north side, steep cliffs alternate with sandy beaches, which are only reachable by sea, since the road ends in Unare. On the south side, plains are host to the towns of Irapa, Marval, San Antonio, and Guiria. The highest elevations are Cerro El Humo, or Smoke Mountain, with an altitude of 1,371 meters, and Cerro Patao, 1,070 meters high. Temperatures range from 15 to 26 C, and the tropical rain forest vegetation here is related to the one found in Amazonas and Guayana.

Near Caripe, we find the Natural Monument named after Alexander Humboldt. The famous caves of the Guacharo are the principal attractions of this park, established in 1949. This cave system is at least 10,200 meters long. The tourist area is 1,200 meters in length and includes three "rooms". A colony of around 10,000 remarkable birds, the guacharos, makes its home in these caves. Similiar to bats, the birds direct their movements according to the echoes of their raucous cries off the cavern walls. The 15,000 hectare area around the cave was made into a National Park in 1975.

The lake of Restinga on the island of Margarita occupies about 100 square Km; its National Park has 10,700 hectares. The lake is distinguished by a labyrinth of mangroves of unusual beauty.

The salt pans of Araya, once protected by a castle now in ruins, the beaches of the gulf of Cariaco, the beaches along Cumana, Puerto La Cruz, and Mochima, among others, are ideal places to enjoy the unpolluted pulchritude of the Caribbean coast.

# GUAYANA

Guayana, with a surface area of 421,000 square kilometers, occupies 46% of the nation's territory, while its population is but 4% of the nation's total. Politically, it comprises the state of Bolivar and the federal territories Amazonas and Delta Amacuro.

Columbus discovered these lands in 1498 on his third voyage. His fleet, originally of six ships, became separated. Three of the vessels came to an island, which was then named Trinidad. Moving westward, the water changed from a transparent blue to a muddy yellow, which led the navigators to deduce the existence of a large, but unseen river. It was the Huyapari, today called the Orinoco.

In 1500, the river was named "sweet river" by Vicente Yañez Pinzon, former captain of the Niña. Diego de Ordaz tried to sail this body of water in 1532 and according to Gonzalo Fernandez de Oviedo y Valdes in his General and Natural History of the Indies: "... they found the river blocked naturally with stones, and it had a great fall, so that it was impossible for the people and the ships to move forward, because the water descends more than two rods and a half or three, and it is almost as wide as a crossbow shot, and the banks are high and made up of broken rocks." After this frustrated attempt, Ordaz went back to Cumana.

In 1533, Alonzo de Herrera, Ordaz's lieutenant, reached the mouth of the Meta. In 1596, Sir Walter Raleigh published his book "The Discovery of the Great and Beautiful Empire of Guayana", a description of what he had seen during his exploration of the Orinoco and lower Caroni, in search of the "El Dorado".

Due to its size, Guayana presents a vast natural, cultural, and historical landscape, unified by the Orinoco, with its high and lower sectors, its delta, and its tributaries such as the Caroni or Cuyuni. Indeed, some would like to call the region Orinoquia.

Man's work is not absent. Guayana hosts Venezuela's heavy industry. The Orinoco steelworks, the Caroni Aluminum Industry, the Cerro Bolivar iron mines, the Guri hydroelectric complex, and the Bauxite mines of los Pijiguaos are the industrial backbone of the country.

History, too, has left its imprint. One can find the buildings which housed the Congress of Angostura and the Correo del Orinoco Journal. each of these stand for important instruments which helped bring about the process of emancipation, reinitiated during the second republic. From here, Bolivar consolidated his forces, and began the campaign which would take him to Bogota and thence to the battlefield of Carabobo, where the military supremacy of the new republic would be established.

One can reach Guayana from the Atlantic, from the Llanos, from the Amazon basin, and from the Esequibo. Historically, the preferred road has been the delta. This aquatic labyrinth consists of some 420 branches, with water flowing upstream or downstream, depending on the six-hour tides. The delta is inhabited by the Warao indians, who shun civilization and live in houses built upon platforms in a no-man's land between jungle and river.

The Orinoco is navigable from the delta until Puerto Ayacucho. Here the waters pass between enormous stones, giving the impression of a giant strainer. These waters form the Atures rapids and divide the lower from the upper Orinoco. The latter is part of the Amazonas Federal Territory, accessible only by river or by air; the former only when the "curiara" or "bongo" is manned by someone wise to the river's whims, since the seasonal rains continually cover and uncover obstacles.

Here nature lives in a climatic community, wherein the native indian is completely integrated. In this tropical rain forest, with 4,000 mm of annual rainfall, plant and animal life feed on each other, alternatively and successively, until the matter and energy chain culminates in what biologists call the climax.

The most extraordinary part of the region is the "Gran Sabana", which is occupied by one of the oldest geological formations on earth, the Guayana massif. This formation is composed of jungles, high plains, and "tepuyes" or high plateaus. The best-known tepuyes are the Auyantepui and the Roraima.

The Auyantepui was first climbed by Felix Cardona Puig in 1947. This tepuy is famous because it is the site of Angel Falls, whose 1,000 meter altitude makes it the highest in the world. It is named after Jimmy Angel, an aviator who landed on top of the mesa in the 1930s. Unable to take off again, he returned to civilization unscathed, but on foot.

The gateway to Angel Falls is Canaima, which is only accessible by air. Then, there is a two day's journey by canoe on the Carrao and Churun rivers, where the launch navigates in rust-colored waters amongst jungle and tepuyes, until the falls appear —the region's most famous attraction— providing a spectacular climax to the trip.

The opposite pole of attraction is provided by Roraima, which entered world literature through Sir Arthur Conan Doyle's novel "The Lost World", published in 1885. Doyle portrayed a remote, unknown, and mysterious region, where time had stopped. The Gran Sabana region has attracted more scientists and explorers than any other in the country, and these scholars have not only contemplated its beauties, but have also poured their experiences into writing. Thus, fiction and reality are as intertwined in the Guayana literature, as is the jungle which inspires it.

# CARACAS

"Caracas, there it is; its red roofs,
its white tower, its blue hills and
its bands of gentle birds
cloud my eyes with tears."

So said the poet Perez Bonalde towards the latter half of the 19th century. To him, Caracas was at once static and dynamic, and the latter element was essential in understanding it.

Diego de Lozada founded the city in 1567, and King Philip II of Spain bestowed upon it its title and coat of arms in 1591. It then became the capital of Venezuela. But initial growth was slow and difficult. In 1578, according to a map drawn up by the Governor, Juan de Pimentel, the city comprised 24 blocks of four houses each. In 1696, its population had reached 6,000. Earthquakes devastated it in 1755, 1812, and again in 1967. A map dated 1722 shows 90 blocks, which represents a quadruplication in about 200 years.

The 1812 earthquake accounts for the fact that our architectural legacy from the colonial past has been reduced. Among the works that have survived, we can single out the Cathedral; the church of San Francisco; the convent of San Francisco (today the Palace of the Academies); the Goverment Palace (today the Casa Amarilla or Yellow House); the churches of Las Mercedes, Altagracia, and Candelaria; Bolivar's house; and the house of the Count of Tovar, today called Quinta Anauco.

In 1870, the city had reached a population of 70,000. It was then that the president, Antonio Guzman Blanco, embarked on an elaborate building program which produced the Palacio Legislativo (Capitol), the original University buildings, the Museum, the Pantheon, the temple of Santa Teresa, the Municipal Theater, the Santa Capilla church, and the Caracas-La Guaira railroad.

After 1900 the importance of oil in the world market began to have its effect on the city, and this was augmented by immigration following the second World War. Caracas has been exposed to an ever-increasing growth, and many of the works of the past have been demolished to make way for widened streets and massive architectural complexes such as El Silencio and Avenida Bolivar, ending recently with the Parque Central, all of which have completely changed the face of the city.

Caracas lies in a valley 25 Km. long and 10 Km. wide. It has mount Avila overlooking it to the north and the Guaire river dividing it in two, and it narrows down gradually at either end.

It began to grow, first to the west with Catia; then towards the southwest with El Paraiso. Next came the developing, neighborhoods of the east: Country Club, Altamira, La Castellana and so on, ending finally with Lagunita and Alto Prado. Since the city cannot grow further horizontally, it is now growing in a vertical direction. This fact has brought the following consequences: while the rest of the country is wide and spacious, the Caraqueño is pressed for space and time. This, however, does not prevent him from always being friendly, courteous and amiable.

The city has representatives of every race under the sun and tends to stratify itself into social classes, which differ not only in wealth but in their basic social characteristics. More than a third of the population, which will reach three million by the end of the century, lives in the so-called marginal sections of the city. These neighborhoods are a consequence of the migratory flow from the country into the city, which is a common phenomenon in South America. It is ironical that these neighborhoods usually have the best view of the city.

There are many places for the "caraqueños" to enjoy nature, such as the Caricuao Zoo, the Paseo de los Proceres, the Botanical Gardens, the Los Caobos Park, and other boulevards and walks. These spots, covered by a luxuriant vegetation which can only be found in the tropics, are complemented by luxurious shopping centers, restaurants of every type of decor and cuisine, and private clubs. The cable car to the Avila, the "teleferico", takes one up in minutes to an elevation of 2,000 meters, where climate and environment change accordingly.

The Caracas subway, the Metro, is slowly easing the tensions caused by the transportation problems common to every big city, and which are even more pronounced in Caracas. This system is moving progressively eastward and southwestward from the center. Not only is it a remarkably efficient public service, but it has contributed to the embellishment of the city with its various architectural works.

With an altitude of 900 meters, Caracas is a tropical city, with a climate poetically described as "eternal springtime". But today it is somewhat warmer than in the past, as nature struggles against the masses of concrete.

In Caracas, one has to learn how to live within the city every day. In spite of its 400 years, this metropolis still resembles a rebellious adolescent, unsatisfied with itself and trying to find its own identity.

But like someone we love, the city generates an almost magical nostalgia. Perhaps it is the brightness, the contrasts, the sense of movement. It is intangible but definite, and its value is felt when we leave.

That is why Bolivar wrote:

> My arms spanned a thousand leagues,
> But my heart will always
> remain in Caracas:
> there I received life
> there I must part with it.

# THE MIDLAND

The Spanish conquistador settled on the coasts, where his ships first landed. Thence, he made his way inland, where he had to deal with the natives, who at times treated him with friendship and sometimes with hostility. The Old World brought new ways: interpreters, friendly indians, commerce, barter, comprehension, and confrontation.

One of the oldest tales of the region dates from 1532, penned by Nicholas Federmann, a lieutenant-governor of the Welser merchant house. Federmann chronicles his expedition from Coro to the plains, in search of the "El Dorado", the city of gold, as well as the Southern Sea, as the Pacific was then called. The diary neglects scenic descriptions, concentrating instead on encounters with the indians, both friendly and unamicable.

Other historians, notably Pedro Simon, Oviedo y Baños, and Alonso de Herrera, also include descriptions of the Central region. As these works testify, colonialization was an arduous task. Cities appeared, but slowly: Barquisimeto in 1552, Valencia in 1555, Los Teques in 1703; Maracay was not even a parish until 1743.

The states of Miranda, Aragua, Carabobo, Yaracuy, and Lara are the center of the country: geographically, economically, and historically. In 1567, the capital of Venezuela shifted from Coro to Caracas. From then on, all roads led to the center, like the spokes of a wheel. The first railways, built in the 19th century, joined Valencia to Caracas, Puerto Cabello to Valencia, Caracas to La Guaira, Carenero to El Guapo, and Barquisimeto to Tucacas. This last-named was the first railway in South America.

The independence movement originated in the center. Here the first and second republics were won and lost, here independence was finally gained in the battle of Carabobo. All the central states except Lara and Yaracuy have access to the sea. The latter two are neighboring states attached to the center for the purposes of this description.

The state of Miranda is named after Francisco de Miranda, who dedicated his entire life to the independence, not only of Venezuela, but of all South America. He designed the national flag, and received the title of "Precursor". This state surrounds the Federal District, and serves as an expansion area and "lungs" for the latter. Close relatives, the Federal District and Miranda even share some public services. Miranda also has Barlovento, a coastal town rich in cocoa, tradewinds, folklore and music.

The coastline stretches from Boca de Uchire to Chuspa. It hosts the beautiful, 30-Km long lake of Tacarigua, now a National Park. This lake has over 1,000 mm. annual precipitation and an average temperature of 24 to 28°C, providing unique conditions for certain tropical plants and animals. Among the vegetation, we single out the Red Mangrove (Rhizophora mangle), Black Mangrove (Avicennmia germinans), and the White

Mangrove (Laguncularia racemosa). Ornithologists will be delighted to find various species of scarlet ibis (Threskiornitidae), flamingos (Phoenicopteridae) and gulls (Laridae), among others.

Aragua is mostly agricultural, but has begun to industrialize since 1960. From a conservationist point of view, it contains the oldest National Park in Venezuela, established in 1937. Originally called "Rancho Grande", it was renamed in honor of Henri pittier, who spent the years from 1930 to 1940 fighting for the preservation of the area. Here one finds varied plant and animal life, notably the tallest tree in Venezuela, the "Cucharon" or "Niño" tree, which can reach heights of 50 meters.

Aragua, Carabobo, and Yaracuy are geographically similar. They are agricultural, and have light and medium industries which are flourishing, especially near the cities of Maracay and Valencia. Poet and writer Luis Pastori has thus described the region: "The valleys are decorated by old Saman trees, like venerable relics; on the mountain sides, the intense yellow of Araguaneyes reverberates, while in the mountains, the Bucares, shading coffee trees, lend their scarlet colors to the romantic fruit of the shrubs below".

The state of Lara has mountainous, desert, and plains regions. Great areas of land are dedicated to sisal and sugar cane plantations, trying to wrest space from the semi-desert, where man and goat hold sway. The goat, seemingly able to exist on anything except rocks, is the basis for a whole system of nutrition and crafts. Its products may be seen along the road from Carora to Barquisimeto, the latter founded in 1552 by Juan de Villegas and whose indian name signifies "ash-colored river".

Evenings near Barquisimeto are ushered in by remarkable sunsets. The setting sun turns the sky red, shading to yellow and finally to blue. It was perhaps this chromatic display which inspired the Larense composer Juan Ramon Barrios to transmute light to sound in his memorable song, "Noches Larenses" (Nights of Lara):

The night is so lovely,
all is calm and silent
our soul is so delighted,
with music of the stars
the moon in all its candor,
filters through the garden
and caresses the rose,
which perfumes the breeze
and beautifies the jasmine.

# THE WEST

On May 18, 1499, an expedition captained by Alonso de Ojeda, accompanied by Juan de La Cosa and the Italian geographer Americo Vespuci, set sail from the port of Santa Catalina de Cadiz, bound for the new world. They sailed up the Orinoco delta, explored the coasts of Paria, and touched at Margarita. Continuing westwards, they came to the coasts of Macarapana, then rounded cape La Vela.

On the 24th of August, they came to a large lake "and found therein, especially on the eastern shore, large indian villages, built out upon waters up to chest depth, with the houses built upon large pilings sunk into the water, using canoes for all their necessities", to quote Fray Pedro Simon in his Second Notice. The scene was reminiscent of Venice, and the area was designated "Little Venice" or Venezuela, whence the present name of the country is derived. The region is currently called Occidente (the West) and is divided into the states of Falcon and Zulia.

Zulia has an identity all of its own. Its hallmarks are its distinctive speech; its music, including the "Gaita", which is now a national Christmas music; and the art of weaving as practiced by the Goajiro indians. These aborigines weave tapestries in a wide variety of colors and designs, in contrast to the monochromatic landscape which they inhabit.

The state of Zulia is placed like a horseshoe around the lake of Maracaibo. A forest of oil wells covers the eastern side, reflecting the activities of modern industry, while the west side is still a reflection of the past. Here, people still live in houses built on stilts, and their activities are fishing and the repair and construction of boats. So it was in the old days, when the lake was the only access to the region and the gateway to the Andes. The state has a rich soil and an intensive agriculture, and it produces over half of the country's oil.

Lake Maracaibo is separated from the Gulf of Venezuela by the Maracaibo bar, a sandbank which must be continually dredged to afford passage to seagoing vessels. To the north, the state of Zulia ends in the Goajira peninsula, a semidesertic land belonging to whoever can live in it. Its inhabitants are the Goajiro indians, who know no borders, whose roof is the sky, whose walls are Cardon cactus, whose neighbors are their family, and whose family is the tribe.

Maracaibo is the state capital. It was founded on August 8, 1529, by Ambrose Alfinger, in one of his infrequent pauses from the relentless pursuit of the "El Dorado", the mythical city of gold. Alfinger was comissioned by the Welsers, a German merchant house, who had obtained a land concession from Charles V of Spain in 1528. Confirmed in 1530, the concession took in all lands "between the cape of La Vela and the gulf of Cariaco".

Until 1962, Maracaibo was relatively isolated from the rest of the country. It was then that the Rafael Urdaneta Bridge was completed, spanning the lake at its narrowest point. Thus, Maracaibo is now part of the national road system and its contact with the rest of the country has increased. The city is gay and colorful, to the point where the famous Venezuelan writer, Romulo Gallegos, dubbed it "the city that never sleeps".

Going east from Zulia, we find Falcon. This state is divided into mountains and deserts. The latter, called the "medanos" of Coro and the Paraguana peninsula, make up Venezuela's contribution to the 3.5 per cent of the American continent occupied by desert.

Paraguana has been called "the heir of the winds" by a poet. Day and night, the winds blow relentlessly across the landscape. The vegetation fights to stay upright, leaving little energy to survive. Clouds unceasingly drift by, as if ignoring the pleas of the parched land below for even one drop of water. Cacti spread their arms in search for moisture, and even dew is welcome. Water is definitively equivalent to life here.

Silence overwhelms even the gusts of wind. The land appears to be defenceless, its fate: to contemplate the passage of the sun. Day after day, sunrise, zenith, and sundown follow each other. The bluish shadows of morning disappear by midday, but return in darker hues at sunset, finally turning black. The moon rises. The wind has not stopped today, nor will it slacken tomorrow. In this inexorable progression, the cacti put out flowers amid their spearlike spines, and birds and bees come to enjoy the nectar... and they all survive. Always, there is hope for a new beginning.

Leaving Paraguana, we come to the city of Coro, the state capital and the first capital of Venezuela. A venerable city, where the air itself brings the memories of a distant and dignified past, with enough time and space for everything. The atmosphere was doubtless the inspiration for Arturo Uslar Pietri's lines, written on the walls of one of the colonial houses:

> "Sun and wind fill the narrow streets of Coro. A narrow edge of shadow falls from the eaves onto the scorched earth. Thick walls of compacted earth protect the houses. Inside, there is a patio, with trees and flowers, surrounded by arcaded corridors. A sense of freshness, as if preserved and decanted, pervades these deep, thick-walled dwellings, where sunlight seems screened and caressing".

# THE PLAINS

"Yo naci en esta ribera del Arauca vibrador..." —I was born on a riverbank of the vibrating Arauca— so begins the second national anthem of Venezuela, the Alma Llanera. The Llanos, the plains that inspired this song fully comprise a third of Venezuela's area and a fifth of its population.

Walled in by the Andes and the northern coastal ranges, these plains are the basins of the major rivers: the Orinoco, the Apure, and the Meta, which flow eastwards towards the sea. These ternary and quaternary lands are traditionally divided into high and low llanos by the hundred-meter height contour line, and are administratively divided into the states of Guarico, Apure, Portuguesa, Barinas and Cojedes.

These states are unified not only by geography, but by a common cultural, historical, and geographical heritage. Indivisible by nature, there are many factors which unite them: climate, vegetation, fauna, and above all, the character of the inhabitants, the llaneros.

With the coming of Columbus, the Llanos experienced cultural and religious colonization, as well as racial mixture between the native Indians, the caucasian Spaniards, and the black African slaves.

In his book "A Voyage to the Equinoctial Regions of the New World", the scientist and explorer Alexander von Humboldt recorded a vivid image of this immense territory: "the imposing spectacle of the starry sky dome in its enormous extension, the fresh breeze which sweeps over the plains at night, the swaying movement of the grass in its higher points, all of this reminded us of the surface of the ocean."

This vision seems to depict all the dimensions of this environment, and, as its product, the llanero. On one hand, the sheer size, the absence of border lines, the lack of any reference points. On the other hand, the harsh contrasts: day and night, flood and drought, life and death.

The terrain, the diversity of plants and animals, the domestic animals and animals domesticated by man, and finally the activities carried out by man, these are all features of the llanos. Man must devise a way of subsisting, of protecting himself from the sun and rain, of relating to others; as a form of continuing the species or simply as a way of spreading out.

Here the rivers give life to man. They are sources of water and of food, and also a route of transportation. But they also harbor dangerous enemies. Fish like the pavon, the coporo, the valenton and the catfish are tasty indeed; but not so the caribe, known also as piranha, with its rows of fearsome teeth, nor the electric eel with its deadly shocks.

The chiguire, the world's largest rodent, is sometimes so abundant that its numbers must be reduced; other species, however, such as the lapa, the danta or tapir, the deer, and the baquiro, must be protected by hunting seasons and other laws.

In the dry season, the lakeshores become veritable meeting places of birds. Among them are the garzas reales, garzones soldados, gabanes, corocoras, colorados, cormoranos, and garzas paleta.

It would seem that nature is permanently struggling between lack and excess. Man has attempted to redress this lack of balance, as he has tried to rope the wild pony which nature here seems to resemble. It was near Calabozo that water, which is so useful when adequately supplied and so harmful when excessive, was first brought under control with a dam. Its surplus waters, as the Old Testament would say, made fat the lean beasts: an almost literal simile in this case. Likewise, the water-control modules on the Apure river act as a compensation chamber for the floodwaters.

The clay or sandy soil of the region allows only grass and occasional low shrubs to grow in this region. Clumps of Moriche palm break the monotony and afford some shelter as well as food.

The llanero is the king of these plains. His life is spent between his hammock and his horse, sometimes varied by the use of a canoe. Hence his stoicism, his great power of endurance, and his skill with anything related to horses and horsemanship. Nowhere were these qualities more evident than during the struggle for independence, for it was the llaneros that fought with Bolivar in the Boyaca campaign and who tilted the balance in the decisive battle of Carabobo.

The llanero eases his loneliness when he gathers with his peers, accompanied by his trusty horse and by his valued possesions: his cuatro, harp, maracas, lasso, and fighting cock. It is at these gatherings that he gives free rein to his feelings, as expressed by the coplas (couplets) such as the following, which is perhaps an epitome of this man of the plains:

On top of the llanos, the palm,
on top of the palm, the sky
on top of my horse, myself
on top of myself, my hat.

# THE ANDES

The spinal cord of the South American continent stretches 9,000 km from Tierra del Fuego in the south all the way up to Venezuela. At an average altitude of some 4,000 meters, it is interrupted by peaks which challenge the most seasoned climber: Aconcagua in Chile, Huila and Sierra Nevada in Colombia, and Bolivar in Venezuela, to name a few over the 5,000 meter line.

The Andes, whose name probably comes from the Inca andenes (terraces) cut into the sides of the mountains, arrive in Venezuela in what is called the Oriental Mountain Range, and comprise the states of Tachira, Merida and Trujillo.

For 15,000 years, the mountains were the preserves of the Timoto-Cuica, Aruaco, Beyote, and Caribe indians. They made their first appearance into recorded writing in the fifteenth century, in a manuscript by friar Pedro Simon, chronicler of the Spanish conquest. Friar Pedro was dazzled by the plantations of corn, cotton, yucca, and other vegetables in terraced plots retained by stone walls, which he described as "steep and inaccessible."

This inaccessibility has had its effect on the economy of the region, as well as on the character of the inhabitants, who are considered disciplined and hard-working. Until 1925, when the trans-andean highway was built, the region was unreachable from the east, and all roads led towards the southern side of the lake of Maracaibo. To get to Caracas, one had to go by lake to Maracaibo and thence to travel by sea, often stopping at Aruba or Curazao. Everything was transported by mules until at the turn of the century, three railroads were built: one which went from the port of Encontrados to Tachira, another from Santa Barbara to El Vigia in Merida, and a third which ran from La Ceiba to Motatan in the state of Trujillo.

The region was almost entirely agricultural. Its main cash crop was coffee, a far from stable commodity whose prices, along with Brazil's competition, kept the region in a permanent state of economic adversity, and more than once led to acute economic depression.

Humboldt mentions the region in his treatise on South American botany as "...extremely harsh solitudes, exposed to the inclemencies of tempests where the softened snows are whirled away; a region lashed day and night by the onset of the winds...". But such a description cannot apply to the Venezuelan Paramos or high passes, for it omits the ecstasy of contemplating meadows carpeted with yellow Frailejon plants, contrasting with crystalline rivers and lakes, and capped by snow-clad mountains where the intense blue sky is unmarked by man's tampering. The velvety Frailejon seems to violate nature's laws since contrary to the rest of the flora, its size increases with the altitude.

The scenic treasures of the region are guarded by the Simon Bolivar Park in the Sierra Nevada, which was created in 1952 and includes within its boundaries Pico Bolivar, with an altitude of 5,007 meters —the highest in Venezuela—, as well as the Humboldt (4,942 meters high), and the Bonpland, 4,883 meters in height. At this elevation we are above the frost line. At 3,600 meters we find the "mountain's eyebrow", as the timberline is called locally, with mean temperatures of 10°C. As we descend, we find the wooded and meadow lands with average temperatures of 15 to 9°C.

The three Andean states —Merida, Tachira and Trujillo— were historically three links in a chain whose ends were attached to different power centers. While Trujillo was attached to the province of Caracas, Merida, which included Tachira, was dependent on Bogota. In 1777, a decree of Charles III placed all three states under the jurisdiction of the Captain-Generalcy of Venezuela.

The andeans have always been involved in power struggles. Even in the times of the crown, a revolt in 1781 had to be suppressed by the Spanish authorities. In 1810, the region embraced the independence movement, with the intention of "lifting its neck and shaking off the yoke of oppression". It suffered severe reprisals in consequence. The seminary, the school, and the Episcopal See were all moved to Maracaibo. Merida was the first city to award Bolivar the title of "Libertador" in 1813.

But not only have "Andinos" opposed crown force they have effectively wielded their own power. More than a third of Venezuela's presidents have come from the Andes.

Today, the traditional agricultural economy is being supplemented by the so-called "stackless industry" of tourism. A cable car, linking the city of Merida with the Espejo peak, is the highest and longest in the world.

Each corner of the Andes has a unique beauty. But to experience the truly sublime, man must cast off the wings which modern transportation affords us, and revert to basics. He must climb up to one of the summits of the magic peaks, the five white eagles of the Venezuelan Andes:

The Bonpland
The Humboldt
The Bolivar
The Toro and
The Leon.

# DER SINN DIESES BUCHES

Vater zu sein, einen Baum zu pflanzen und ein Buch zu schreiben gelten als drei Errungenschaften eines erfüllten Lebens. Zur vollkommenen Verwirklichung bedarf es jedoch einer künstlerischen Äusserung, die ich durch dieses Buch zu erreichen versuche.

Die Fotografie hält das Bild nicht nur in Raum und Zeit fest, sondern bezeichnet es auch. Wenn es sich, wie in diesem Fall, um die optische Zusammenfassung eines Landes handelt, beeinflusst diese Bewertung zwangsläufig die visuelle Auffassung desselben und schliesslich auch die Begründung der Werte, auf denen der Patroitismus sich aufbaut und die für die Existenz einer Nation unerlässlich sind. Das war auch meine Absicht.

Venezuela ist gleichzeitig karibisch, amazonisch und Andenland. Seine geologische Bildung reicht vom Quartär bis ins Primär. Dadurch ist es ein von der Natur ausserordentlich reich ausgestattetes Land. Es erstreckt sich wie in sieben Dimensionen durch seine Küsten, das Meer und die Inseln, die Flüsse, die Urwälder, die Hochebenen, die Wüsten, die Tiefebenen und die Berge.

Es war mein Vorsatz, dieses Land mit seinen Stränden, seinem Sand und seinen Palmen —dort wo das Blau mit dem Türkis zusammentrifft— zu zeigen. Ich wollte die Tepuyes, die Tafelberge, näherbringen und mich in der Gran Sabana, der grossen Savanne, erweitern. Ich wollte das Gefühl des Orinoco und des Urwaldes vermitteln. Ich bin durch die Wüsten gezogen um den Kampf ums Überleben zu beobachten. Ich habe die Llanos, die Tiefebenen, überflogen um mich davon zu überzeugen, dass es hinter dem Horizont noch einen Horizont gibt, und hinter diesem noch einen anderen. Ich bin in den Anden gewesen um an der harten täglichen Arbeit teilzuhaben und um das mit dem Himmelsblau eins werdende Grün zu bewundern. Ich habe die Städte aus der Luft und vom Boden aus betrachtet, die Orte, die Wolken, den Baum, den Wald und den Berg wahrgenommen. Ich wollte Venezuela mit der Linse malen, so wie es mir am besten gefällt; und habe dabei abstrahiert, vereinfacht, geordnet, um das zu erfassen, was mir gefällt, was nachahmenswert und erhaltenswert ist, was begeistert, erfreut und erhebt.

Mein Beitrag sollte die Schönheit hervorheben, die Dinge in ihrer besten Form und vielleicht in ihrem besten Moment festhalten. Ich wollte das Wichtige, das was über den Eindruck des ersten Moments hinausgeht, bewahren, um das Wesentliche, das Absolute hervorzuheben. Und auf diese Weise wollte ich die Aesthetik, diese schaffende Energie der Proportionen, das Gleichgewicht, das Fehlen des Überflüssigen und des Irrationalen, das Fehlen des Unbarmherzigen und des Unnützen und das Fehlen der Kraft als Ersatz der Vernunft herbeiführt, ergreifen.

Und mit dieser Absicht überlasse ich Ihnen, lieber Leser, diese Bilder, die bisher meine waren und die hoffentlich jetzt Ihre werden.

Gabriel Gazsó

## ZEUGEN DER ZUKUNFT

Dieses weite Land mit seinen 916.445 Quadratkilometern Fläche trägt seit 1501 den Namen Venezuela, der von dem Kartographen Juan de la Cosa in das erste Bildnis Amerikas an dieser Stelle eingetragen wurde und somit in das Imago Mundi, in die grosse Weltkarte, einging. Der Name besiegelte die Identität des Landes mit der Geburtsurkunde vom 27. März 1528, der Real Cédula (königlichen Order), das Rechtsmittel durch welches die Provinz Venezuela ins Leben gerufen wurde. Der Küste entlang von Cabo de la Vela bis Cumaná, tief ins Land hinein von Norden nach Süden, bis zur Quelle des Orinoco, bis an das linke Flussufer heran. Die Casanare-Ebenen, die gesamte Guajira-Halbinsel, ein ganzes Land. Venezuela festigt sich mit dem Titel der Provinzialverwaltung und der Statthalterschaft, Zelle der politisch-territorialen Auffassung innerhalb der juristischen Ordnung der es angehört, dem Staat Spanien.

Rund um dieses im Rahmen der spanischen Kultur und Zivilisation geschaffenen Venezuela entstehen und wachsen andere Provinzen, Provinzialverwaltungen und Statthalterschaften, die ihm in zivilisierendem Rang und in politischer Kategorie gleich sind: Margarita, 1525; Cumaná, 1568; Trinidad, 1591; Guayana, 1568 und die Provinz La Grita-Mérida-Maracaibo, die sich von 1575 bis 1678 entwickelt bis sie schliesslich ab letztgenanntem Datum als Provinzialverwaltung Maracaibo gefestigt wird.

Drei Jahrhunderte lang nimmt die Zivilisation und die Kultur spanischen Ursprungs Formen an im venezolanischen Land bis sie schliesslich die Farbe, die Nuance des Venezolanertums erhält. Während des 18. Jahrhunderts festigt sich die ehemalige Provinz von 1528, nicht nur weil ihr Volk einheimischer wird, sich durch das Kreuzen der Rassen verwurzelt, sich in ihren Städten kultiviert und sich an die zivilen Bräuche und Gepflogenheiten gewöhnt, sondern auch weil sie eigenes Land erhält. Mit starken gesetzlichen Scharnieren schliessen sich ihr alle Territorien aus ihrem Umland und die anderen, bisher zerstreuten Provinzen an. Diese gesetzlichen Scharniere sind die Intendantur des Heeres und die königliche Finanzverwaltung, die 1776 ins Lebens gerufen wurde, die Statthalterschaft von 1777, das königliche Provinzgericht in Caracas von 1786 und das königliche Konsulat von 1792, vier juristische und verwaltungspolitische Einrichtungen deren Sinn es war, das Territorium zu einer einzigen Regierung unter dem Namen Venezuela zu vereinigen. Dank dieses Knotens im Vereinigungsprozess des 18. Jahrhunderts ist es in der Verfassung von 1811 möglich, eine einzige Republik zu schaffen, und kann die gegenwärtige Verfassung, von 1961, in Artikel 7 festhalten: "Das Staatsgebiet entspricht dem der Statthalterschaft Venezuelas vor der 1810 begonnenen politischen Umwandlung, mit den sich aus den rechtskräftig durch die Republik abgeschlossenen Abkommen ergebenden Änderungen". Das Staatsgebiet der Statthalterschaft und des königlichen Provinzgerichts umfasste tatsächlich 1.116.461 Quadratkilometer. Während der Republik erfuhr das Land eine mehr als beträchtliche Verkleinerung. Aber noch ist das Land weit, noch ist es der Aufenthaltsort des Venezolaners, der fünfhundert Jahre ununterbrochene Tradition geerbt hat.

Das Antlitz der Menschen spiegelt das Gesicht der Erde wieder. Auf venezolanischem Boden gediehen zahlreiche indianische

Kulturen. Seit fünfzehn Jahrtausenden vor Christus sind hier die verschiedensten Stimmen zu hören gewesen. Nicht nur die Barrancas-Kultur an den Ufern des Orinoco, die von dem Anthropologen Mario Sanoja Obediente identifiziert wurde, sondern auch viele andere, schon bekannte oder sich in der Studienphase befindliche im ganzen Land. Die Bücher des Meisters Miguel Acosta Saignes und die zahlreichen archäologischen, ethnologischen und linguistischen Untersuchungen lassen schon von früher die reiche Anwesenheit des Homo venezuelanensis spüren; schon wesentlich eher als der derzeitige Zivilisationsprozess, der 1501 mit der Gründung von Santa Cruz am Venezuela-Golf in der Bucht von Castilletes begann.

Der alte Mensch, der Vertreter dieser Kulturen die in den Fluss der kreolischen Kultur einflossen, der wir heute angehören, ist noch gegenwärtig. Es verbleiben noch ca. achtzehn Völkerstämme, obwohl die offiziellen Zahlen nicht mit denen der Anthropologen übereinstimmen. Demnach müsste es noch zwischen 75.000 und 350.000 Indianer im Lande geben, wahrlich eine Minderheit gegenüber dem Grossteil der Bevölkerung: 14.570.085 Einwohner nach der Volkszählung von 1981, vieleicht 0,9% - weit weniger als der Anteil der ausländischen Kolonien, der sich auf 10% beläuft.

Die lebendigen, in der Minderheit bestehenden indianischen Kulturen haben aber eine andere wichtige Bedeutung in der Bildung des jetzigen Venezolaners; sie sind ein wesentlicher Bestandteil unseres Mischungsprozesses, der schon im 17. Jahrhundert begann, zusammen mit dem schwarzen Blut das hier als Sklaventum eintraf. Aus diesen Mischungen entstammt das Volk Venezuelas, wobei die spanische Kultur vorherrscht. Daher ist die Landessprache auch Spanisch.

Das politisch vereinte Volk Venezuelas im 18. Jahrhundert ist auch eine soziale und kulturelle Einheit. Die Soziologie unterstreicht die Gegenwart des Mestizen oder Kreolen, der damals "Pardo" —Brauner— genannt wurde. Im Jahre 1800 zählte Venezuela rund eine Million Einwohner. Davon waren zu der Zeit achthunderttausend schon kreolische Venezolaner, unmöglich nach Kasten, Hautfarbe oder kulturellem Verhalten zu unterscheiden; und der Rest, Weisse, Schwarze, Indianer, befand sich bereits im Anpassungsprozess. Diese Anpassung wird schliesslich während des 19. Jahrhunderts voll und ganz erreicht, als das Volk immer tiefer ins Land zieht, mit dem Feldbau beginnt, sich dem Land anpasst, das Venezolanertum vertieft.

Im tiefen Land der wahre Venezolaner, dieser alte, fast fünfhundert jährige, von der Sonne gegerbte, von der historischen Witterung umwehte Mensch. Das ist die Mehrheit der durch die Sprache, die Eigentümlichkeit, die Religion, die Gewohnheiten und die Bräuche vereinten Menschen, die in den Orten, Dörfern und Städten des 16. Jahrhundert erhalten blieben. Die neue Mischung, zu der hauptsächlich Spanier, Italiener, Portugiesen und andere Lateinamerikaner beitragen, verstärkt die alte Mischung. Das venezolanische Volk ist 5 Jahrhunderte alt. Es ist ein Volk mit traditioneller Kultur, Bestandteil der sogenannten westlichen und christlichen Zivilisation, aber geschichtlich befindet sich die venezolanische Kultur auf einer Linie mit der intelektuellen und zivilisierenden greco-lateinischen

Tradition, gefärbt durch die Mischung und das Aufeinandertreffen der indianischen Kulturen ihres Gebiets und einiger afrikanischer Kulturen. Die Identität befindet sich in der spanischen Sprache, der offiziellen Landessprache laut dem Grundgesetz.

Die moderne Geschichte Venezuelas umfasst die 50 Jahre zwischen 1936 und 1986. In dieser Zeit hat sich das Land gefestigt und verändert. Es hat sich in seiner Eigenschaft als Volk mit Traditionen gefestigt, der Mischungsprozess wurde besiegelt, es kam das Bewusstsein der Zugehörigkeit auf. Innerhalb der ihm eigenen historischen Strömung hat das Land sich physisch und geistig verändert.

Im Jahr 1936 öffnete sich Venezuela den modernen Ausdrucksströmungen und der modernen Daseinsform als Volk. Die Modernisierung fand nicht, wie es hätte sein sollen, im 19. Jahrhundert statt, sondern erst in der modernen Geschichte. In der Politik gewann die Demokratie die bittere Schlacht zwischen Demokratie und Diktatur. Zunächst eine liberale Demokratie in den Regierungsperioden von 1936-1941 (Eleazar López Contreras) und 1941-1945 (Isaías Medina Angarita), und später die repräsentative Demokratie die das Land ununterbrochen seit 1958 bis heute erlebt. Seit die Wirtschaft durch die Erdölförderung und die Industrialisierung gekennzeichnet wurde, hörte die landwirtschaftliche Tradition aus früheren Jahren —16. bis 19. Jahrhundert— auf. Die Sozialen Veränderungen verwurzeln sich auch in diesen letzten 50 Jahren: das ländliche Volk wird zum Stadtvolk; durch Fortschritte im Gesundheitswesen gelingt es die Kindersterblichkeit zu vermindern und die Lebenserwartung zu erhöhen; der Analphabetenanteil von 90% im Jahre 1936 sinkt 1986 auf 12%; das systematische, durch den Staat gelenkte Erziehungswesen wächst bis zur Verallgemeinerung, 98,5% der Bevölkerung zwischen 7 und 13 Jahren geht zur Schule; damals gab es zwei Universitäten, heute sind es 97 Hochschulen. Die Zeichen des Fortschritts sind im Städtebau zu erkennen. Nachdem die alten Kolonialbauten abgerissen und die Städte vollkommen neu aufgebaut wurden, wird die Silhouette von Caracas, Maracaibo, Valencia, San Cristóbal jetzt von Hochhäusern geprägt. Jede kleine Stadt ist mit der mühseligen Arbeit der Modernisierung beschäftigt.

Die Modernisierung ist natürlich nicht nur eine rein materielle Angelegenheit grosser Strassen, Staudämme, Industrien sondern hauptsächlich eine kulturelle Beschäftigung. Schule, Universität, Kleinbetrieb, Wissenschaft, Technologie, Technik, sie alle beruhen auf der Fähigkeit, sich zu modernisieren. Die Festigung der Demokratie, die Umwandlung des Staates, die Möglichkeit, die Auslandsschuld zu verkraften, die Findung einer der Gegenwart und der Zukunft angepassten Wirtschaft, alles hängt von den kulturellen Fähigkeiten des Volkes ab. Die Zukunftsgeschichte, die Geschichte der nächsten hundert Jahre, wird darüber richten ob Venezuela tatsächlich die Modernität erreicht hat. In der Zwischenzeit ist dieser Bildband ein Zeuge davon, wie das Land und der Mensch für die Zukunft gerüstet sind.

Guillermo Morón

# DIE GEGENDEN VENEZUELAS

# DER OSTEN

Es war im Jahre 1498, am dritten August und während der dritten Reise, die Admiral Christoph Kolumbus zu den Westindischen Inseln unternahm. Er befand sich an Bord seines Lieblingsschiffes, der Niña, ursprünglich Santa Clara genannt, 36 Meter lang, 11 Meter breit, drei Masten von je 22, 18 und 11 Metern Höhe, mit viereckigen, weissen Segeln —auf jedem Segel ein rotes Kreuz— ausgestattet.

Der Admiral, der sich auf dem Weg von der Insel Trinidad zu den trüben Gewässern der Boca de Dragón, der Drachenmündung, befand, um dort an dem Flecken zu landen, den er Isla de Gracia getauft hatte, war bei Macuro angelangt, auf der Maracapana-Halbinsel, die heute Paria heisst und von der damals geglaubt wurde, dass es eine Insel ist.

Es war aber eine echte Insel, Cubagua genannt, auf der durch eine Verpflanzung der politischen und sozialen Strukturen Spaniens, unter der Herrschaft Ferdinand V. und Isabella I. von Kastilien, im Jahre 1500 die Stadt Nueva Cádiz als erste Stadt auf dem südamerikanischen Kontinent gegründet wurde. Dort entsteht eine städtebauliche Struktur quadratisch angeordneter Strassen, mit Rathaus, Kirche, königlichem Schatzamt, Geschäften und Wohnhäusern, die 1523 ihren Titel als Stadt erhält.

Im Jahre 1538 erlies Königin Doña Juana in Valladolid die erste Stadtverordnung Venezuelas, in der Satzungen enthalten waren, die auch heute noch für jeden Naturschützer Geltung haben:

> "Keiner darf ohne Erlaubnis am Strand oder in den Strassen Baugruben graben; der Abfall darf weder auf der Strasse noch am Strand abgeladen werden; kein Schiff darf die Insel ohne Erlaubnis verlassen, ausser denen, die nach Margarita fahren; und die Händler, die sich nicht dem offiziellen Satz unterwerfen, werden ihre Ware los", um nur einige zu zitieren.

Nueva Cádiz wurde auf der Insel Cubagua erbaut, wo es weder Wasser noch Vegetation oder Tiere gab. Ihr Lebensunterhalt bestand aus dem einzigen erneuerbaren —aber nie erneuerten— Naturprodukt: Perlen. Als die Austernbänke schwanden verfiel die Wirtschaft, wurde die Bevölkerung weniger, bis schliesslich 1543 ein Tropensturm die Stadt niederfegt.

Zu diesem Zeitpunkt war der spanische Konquistador bereits seit fast einem halben Jahrhundert auf dem Kontinent, und in der Zeit hatte er eine Festung in der Neverí-Mündung erbaut um die Wasserversorgung der Insel Cubagua zu gewährleisten, Expeditionen flussaufwärtes des Orinoco und des Meta unternommen, die Indianer in der christlichen Lehre unterrichtet, sie zu Sklaven gemacht oder vernichtet - je nach Denkensart, Laune oder Anweisung des jeweiligen Machthabers.

Der Osten Venezuelas erlebt diverse Epochen: die Entdeckung, die Eroberung, die Kolonisierung, die Befreiung, die Bürgerkriege, die auf der Landwirtschaft ruhende Zeitspanne, das Erdölzeitalter um schliesslich zu einer neuen Wirklichkeit zu gelangen: der Touristik. Hierfür sind gerade im Osten Venezuelas natürliche Bedingungen wie in keinem anderen Gebiet des Landes gegeben.

Unter dem gemeinsamen Nenner Oriente, dem Osten, wird das Land in die Bundesstaaten Anzoátegui, Sucre, Nueva Esparta und Monagas aufgeteilt. Mit Ausnahme des Bundesstaates Monagas sind alle anderen Staaten Küstenstaaten, und der Bundesstaat Nueva Esparta ist ein Inselstaat, gebildet durch die Inseln Margarita, Coche und Cubagua. Die Wirtschaft der Region beruht auf der Landbestellung, dem Fischfang, der Erdölförderung, der Zement- und anderen Industrien. Auf dem landwirtschaftlichen Sektor beträgt die Kakaoernte 50% und die Kaffeernte 14% des Landesgesamts.

Vier Gebiete dieser Region wurden zu Nationalparks —Naturschutzgebieten— erklärt: La Restinga, Mochima, el Guácharo und die Paria-Halbinsel. Dadurch werden diese Gebiete zu einer Art "unantastbarer Zone", deren Ursprung in dem naturschutzfreundlichen Willen Simón Bolívars zu finden ist und in den "Massnahmen zur Erhaltung und zum gewissenhaften Gebrauch der Gewässer" zum Ausdruck gebracht wird. Dieses 1825 in Chuquisaca, Bolivien, erlassene Dokument handelt in seinem Paragraphen 3 über "Schaffung, Gedeihen und Bestimmung der Wälder".

Im Jahre 1978 wurde ein 37.500 ha grosses Gebiet auf der Paria-Halbinsel zum Nationalpark erklärt. Dieser Park erstreckt sich von Cabo Tres Puntas bis Punta de Peñas an der östlichen Spitze der Halbinsel. Die Nordseite endet an abrupt abfallenden Steilküsten, die durch kleine, nur von See her zugängliche Sandstrände unterbrochen werden. Da die Strasse in dem Ort Unare aufhört, bleibt nur noch der Luft- oder Seeweg. Im Süden erstrekken sich Ebenen und die Ortschaften Irapa, Marval, San Antonio, Yoco und Güiria. Die Berge El Humo (1.371 m) und Patao (1.070) sind die höchsten in diesem Gebiet, wo die Temperatur zwischen 15 und 26 Grad Celsius schwankt. Die Flora besteht im wesentlichen aus Tropen —und Regenwald und die Fauna ähnelt jener der Amazonas— und Guayana-Gebiete.

Die Cueva del Guácharo —Guácharo-Höhle—, in der Nähe von Caripe gelegen, wurde 1949 zum Naturdenkmal Alexander von Humboldt erklärt, dem Mann zu Ehren, der sie für die Welt entdeckte. Es handelt sich um ein 10.200 Meter tiefes Höhlensystem, dessen "touristischer" Teil 1.200 Meter entlang dreier "Säle" verläuft. Eine Kolonie von etwa 10.000 Guácharo-Vögeln, die im Höhleneingang leben und sich an dem Echo ihres Krächzens orientieren, stellt die Hauptattraktion dar und gibt einem 15.000 Ha grossen, rund um die Höhle geschaffenen Nationalpark seinen Namen.

Die auf der Insel-Margarita gelegene Lagune La Restinga nimmt eine Fläche von 10.700 ha ein. Die Lagune selbst ist 100 $km^2$ gross und beherbergt ein landschaftlich reizvolles Mangrovenlabyrinth.

Die Salinen in Araya mit den Ruinen des zu ihrem Schutz erbauten Kastells, die Strände des Cariaco-Golfes und die zwischen Cumaná, Puerto La Cruz und Mochima gelegenen Buchten bieten Gelegenheit, diese makellosen Küsten zu geniessen.

## GUAYANA

Mit seinen 421.000 km$^2$ nimmt Guayana 46% der Gesamtfläche Venezuelas ein, beherbergt aber nur 4% seiner Bevölkerung. Nach der politischen Unterteilung des Landes nimmt Guayana die Bundesterritorien Amazonas und Delta Amacuro sowie den Bundesstaat Bolívar ein.

Im Jahre 1498, bei seiner dritten Reise zu den Westindischen Inseln, trennt Kolumbus seine aus sechs Schiffen bestehende Flotille. Drei davon landen auf einer Insel die den Namen Trinidad erhält. Von dort westwärts fahrend wechselt das Wasser von klarem Blau zu trübem Gelb, was den Beobachter die Gegenwart eines wasserreichen Flussen vermuten lässt, den er nie zu sehen bekommt. Es war der Huyapari, heute Orinoco genannt.

Im Jahre 1500 wird der Fluss von Vicente Yáñez Pinzón, dem ehemaligen Kapitän der "La Niña", "Río Dulce" - "der süsse Fluss" genannt. Gemäss den Erzählungen des Gonzalo Fernández de Oviedo y Valdés in seiner Allgemeinen- und Naturgeschichte der Westindischen Inseln versucht Diego de Ordaz 1532, flussaufwärts zu fahren: "und sie fanden den Fluss auf natürliche Weise durch Felsen unterbrochen, und er fällt in einem grossen Wasserfall, so dass es Schiffen und Menschen unmöglich war, fortzufahren, weil das Wasser aus mehr als zweieinhalb oder drei Stadien Höhe wie aus einem Mühlwehr fällt, breit fast wie ein Armbrustschuss weit, und an den Seiten nur hohe Felsklippen." Nach diesem missglückten Versuch kehrt Ordaz nach Cumaná zurück.

Im Jahre 1533 gelangt Alonzo de Herrera, Stellvertreter des Ordaz, bis zur Mündung des Meta-Flusses. Im Jahre 1596 veröffentlicht Sir Walter Raleigh in England das Buch über "Die Entdeckung des Grossen und Herrlichen Reiches von Guayana", als Erzählung dessen, was er auf der Suche nach dem "El Dorado" auf seiner Reise über den Orinoco und den Unterlauf des Caroní gesehen und erlebt hatte.

Aufgrund ihrer Weite schliesst die Guayana-Region eine umfangreiche Naturzenerie, mit viel Geschichte und Kultur, zusammen. Das ganze Gebiet wird durch den Orinoco —sei es nun sein Ober— oder Unterlauf, das Delta oder seine Zuflüsse wie der Caroní oder der Cuyuní - zusammengefasst. Aus diesem Grunde wird das Gebiet auch gerne Orinoquia genannt.

Was das durch Menschen Geschaffene betrifft, so beherbergt Guayana die Schwerindustrie Venezuelas. Die Orinoco-Hütte, das Caroní-Aluminiumwerk, der Eisenbaubetrieb am Bolívarberg und der hydroelektrische Komplex Guri sind die grössten Industriebetriebe des Landes.

Als Zeugen historischer Geschehnisse verbleiben heute noch die Bauten, die den Angostura-Kongress und die "Correo del Orinoco"-Zeitung, die der Befreiungsbewegung, welche der zweiten Republik wieder begann, den notwendigen und in der Zeit angebrachten Aufschwung gaben. Ab diesem Moment gelingt es Bolívar, die für den Feldzug, der ihn bis nach Bogotá führen sollte um von dort aus zum Schlachtfeld von Carabobo zurückzukehren, notwendigen Kräfte unter seiner Herrschaft zu vereinen um die so notwendige militärische Übermacht zu definieren, die für die Festigung der jungen Republik benötigt wird.

Guayana ist vom Atlantik, von den Llanos, —der Tiefebene— vom Amazonas und vom Esequibo aus zu erreichen. Die historische Einfahrt vom Meer aus in das Gebiet bildet das Delta. Dieses Wasserlabyrinth besteht aus etwa 420 Flussarmen, deren Gewässer je nach den Gezeiten im 6-Stunden-Rythmus flussaufwärts oder flussabwärts fliessen.

Die Gegend wird von den Warao-Indianern bewohnt, die, mit nur wenig Kontakt zur Zivilisation, in Pfahlbauten hausen, auf einem Streifen gebaut, der nicht mehr ganz Fluss und weder Urwald ist.

Der Orinoco ist vom Delta bis nach Puerto Ayacucho schiffbar, wo das Wasser durch enorme Felsen, einem gigantischen Sieb gleicht fliesst: die Stromschnellen von Atures, die das Gebiet in oberen und unteren Orinoco teilen. Erstgenannter bildet das Bundesterritorium Amazonas, welches nur auf dem Luft und dem Flussweg zu erreichen ist. In letztem Fall fährt man in Bongos oder Curiaras —Einbäumen— die unbedingt von einem Kenner der Eigentümlichkeiten des Flusses geführt werden müssen. Je nach Wasserspiegel bedecken oder entblössen die Gewässer Felsen, Steine und Landstriche.

Die Natur lebt in einer klimatischen Gemeinschaft in der auch der Indianer integriert ist. In einem hydrophilen, megathermischen Urwald mit einem Regenfall von ca. 4.000 mm im Jahr, dienen sich Tier- und Pflanzenwelt abwechselnd und aufeinanderfolgend als Nahrung, bis sich die Energie- und Materieübertragung stabilisiert um das was die Botaniker Klimax nennen, zu erreichen.

Das ausserordentlichste Gebiet dieser Region ist die Gran Sabana —die grosse Savanne— die eine der ältesten geologischen Formationen der Welt darstellt: das Guayana-Massiv. Hier sind Hochebenen, Urwald und die Tepuyes —Tafelberge— anzutreffen. Die bekanntesten Tafelberge sind der Auyantepuy und der Roraima.

Der Auyantepuy wurde zum ersten Mal im Jahre 1947 von Félix Cardona Puig erklommen. Dieser Tepuy ist bekannt, da an seinem Hang der höchste Wasserfall der Welt, der 1.000 Meter hohe Salto Angel —benannt nach dem Piloten Jimmy Angel, der nach einer Landung auf dem Gipfel des Auyantepuy von dort nicht mehr starten konnte und zu Fuss in die Zivilisation zurückkehren musste— in die Tiefe stürzt.

Das Eingangstor zum Salto Angel ist Canaima, welches nur auf dem Luftweg zu erreichen ist. Nach zwei Tagen Bootsfahrt auf den Flüssen Churún und Carrao, durch eisenhaltiges, rötliches Wasser, zwischen Tepuys und Urwald hindurch, erreicht man den Höhepunkt einer Reise in diese Region: den Fuss des Angel-Falls.

Die andere Attraktion, der Roraima, ist durch den Roman "Der Kristallberg" von Sir Arthur Conan Doyle aus dem Jahre 1885 in die Weltliteratur eingegangen. Der Autor hat dort einen durch die Abgelegenheit, die Unbekanntheit, das Geheimnisvolle und das Zeitlose gekennzeichneten Schauplatz gefunden. Wie kein anderes Gebiet hat die Gran Sabana die Aufmerksamkeit der Wissenschaftler und Expeditionsführer auf sich gezogen. Diese Besucher haben nicht nur den Anblick des Naturschauspiels genossen, sondern auch ihre Erlebnisse niedergeschrieben. Daher sind auch in der Literatur über Guayana, ähnlich wie im Dschungel, Wahrheit und Dichtung oft ineinander verschlungen.

# CARACAS

"Caracas, da ist es; seine roten Dächer,
sein weisser Turm, seine blauen Hügel,
und seine Schwärme scheuer Tauben
benebeln meine Augen mit Tränen".

So ersinnt der Dichter Pérez Bonalde die Stadt gegen Mitte des vorigen Jahrhunderts, sowohl in statischer als auch in dynamischer Form, denn ohne diese leztgenannte Dimension ist die Stadt unerdenklich und unverständlich.

In 1567 von Diego de Losada gegründet, erhielt es in 1591 von Philipp II Urkunde und Wappen. Caracas ist die Hauptstadt Venezuelas. Das anfängliche Wachstum war langsam und beschwerlich. Nach einem Plan des Gouverneurs Juan de Pimentel zählte die Stadt im Jahre 1578 24 Blocks mit je 4 Häusern. Im Jahre 1696 erreicht sie 6.000 Einwohner. Ein erstes Erdbeben zerstört Caracas 1755, ein zweites 1812 und 1967 wird es abermals erschüttert. Ein 1772 zusammengestellter Stadtplan weist bereits 90 Blocks auf, was einer Vervierfachung in den vergangenen 200 Jahren entspricht.

Hauptsächlich wegen des zweiten Erdbebens ist auf architektonischem Gebiet wenig aus der Kolonialzeit erhalten geblieben. Aus dieser Zeit stammen folgende, erwähnenswerte Gebäude: die Kathedrale; die St. Franziskus-Kirche; das St. Franziskus-Kloster, heute Palast der Akademien; die Kirchen Las Mercedes, Altagracia und Candelaria; das Geburtshaus Simón Bolívars und die Residenz der Grafen von Tovar, heute Quinta Anauco, das Kolonialmuseum.

Im Jahre 1870 zählt die Stadt 48.000 Einwohner. Während der Regierungsperiode des Präsidenten Antonio Guzmán Blanco werden, unter anderem, das Kapitol, die Universität, das Museum, das Pantheon, der Tempel der Heiligen Theresa, das Stadttheater, die Santa Capilla-Kirche und die Eisenbahn zwischen Caracas und La Guaira gebaut.

Aufgrund der Erscheinung des Erdöls in der venezolanischen Wirtschaft und der durch den zweiten Weltkrieg hervorgerufenen Einwanderung, ist die Stadt ab 1900 einem immer schnelleren Wachstum ausgesetzt gewesen. Die Bauwerke der Vergangenheit mussten grossen, breiten Strassen und Baukomplexen wie El Silencio, das Simón Bolívar-Zentrum und schliesslich Parque Central weichen, wodurch das Stadtbild vollkommen verändert wurde.

Langsam wird dieses 25 km von Ost nach West und 10 km von Süd nach Nord messende Tal, das im Norden durch den Avila-Berg, der ihm Sauerstoff spendet, abgegrenzt ist und das durch den Guaire-Fluss geteilt wird, zu eng. Zunächst erweitert sich die Stadt nach Westen mit der Entstehung von Catia, später nach Südwesten —El Paraíso— und schliesslich spriessen im Osten neue Wohngebiete: Country Club, Altamira, La Castellana und so weiter, bis sie schliesslich bei La Lagunita und Alto Prado endet. Nachdem eine horizontale Ausbreitung nunmehr aus Platzmangel unmöglich ist, wächst die Stadt in die Höhe. Dies hat zur Folge, dass der Bewohner von Caracas, der Caraqueño, im Gegensatz zum Rest des Landes wo alles weitläufig und grosszügig angelegt ist, ständig unter Platz und Zeitmangel leidet, was ihn jedoch keineswegs daran hindert freundlich und höflich zu sein.

Ausser dass sich in der Stadt Vertreter jeder nur erdenklichen Menschenrasse zuhause fühlen, ist auch eine Tendenz zur Bildung von Schichten zu beobachten, die sich nicht nur durch ihr Einkommen sondern auch durch tiefe soziale Grundzüge voneinander unterscheiden.

Mehr als ein Drittel einer Bevölkerung, die im letzten Jahrzehnt des 20. Jahrhunderts 3 Millionen Einwohner erreichen wird, lebt in den sogenannten "Barrios" am Rande der Stadt. Diese Elendsviertel sind die Folge der in Südamerika so häufigen Völkerwanderung vom Lande in die Stadt. Es ist eine Ironie des Schicksals, dass gerade diese Wohnviertel den besten Ausblick auf die Hauptstadt geniessen.

Der Caricuao-Zoo und der Parque del Este, der Paseo de Los Próceres, der Botanische Garten, der Park Los Caobos und andere Boulevards und Fussgängerzonen bieten den Einwohnern die Gelegenheit, inmitten der reichhaltigen Vegetation die nur in den Tropen zu finden ist an der frischen Luft zu sein. Luxuriöse Einkaufszentren, Restaurants mit exquisiter Küche und Dekoration, private Clubs aller Art geben Gelegenheit zur Freizeitgestaltung, die das Leben menschlicher macht. Mit der Seilbahn ist man in wenigen Minuten auf dem 2.000 Meter hohen Avila —in einer ganz anderen Atmosphäre und einem wesentlich frischeren Klima.

Die durch den beschwerlichen Transport von einem Platz zum anderen der Stadt und die niedrige Nutzbarkeit der Zeit, die zwar in jeder Grosstadt anzutreffen sind aber in Caracas noch ausgeprägter erscheinen, verursachten Spannungen werden nach und nach durch die Metro, die Untergrundbahn, gemildert. Die U-Bahn verbindet den Westen mit dem Osten, die Stadtmitte mit dem Südwesten, und dieses Massentransportmittel stellt nicht nur ein ausserordentlich wirksames öffentliches Verkehrsmittel dar, sondern hat auch durch zahlreiche Bauten zur Humanisierung der Hauptstadt beigetragen.

In 900 Meter Höhe gelegen ist Caracas eine tropische Stadt mit einem Klima, das von Dichtern als "ewiger Frühling" bezeichnet wurde. Heutzutage ist es etwas wärmer aufgrund des Kampfes zwischen der einst dichteren und zahlreicheren Vegetation und dem Beton.

Caracas ist eine Metropole mit der man jeden Tag aufs neue das Miteinanderleben erlernen muss. Obwohl sie mittlerweile über 400 Jahre alt ist, ist sie weiterhin halbwüchsig und unreif, aufgedreht und unruhig, und in diesem steten Wechsel scheint es so, als ob die Stadt in einem Stadium ständiger Unzufriedenheit nie zu sich selbst finden würde.

Und trotzdem weckt diese Stadt eine fast magische Sehnsucht. Vielleicht ist es ihre Beleuchtung, ihre Kontraste, ihre permanente Bewegung. Sie ist unberührbar und zugleich definiert, und ihr Wert steigt sobald man sie nicht mehr hat: es ist wie mit den Lieben.

Es hatte schon etwas auf sich als Bolívar schrieb:

> "Meine Arme können tausen Meilen weit sein,
> aber mein Herz wird
> immer in Caracas bleiben:
> dort begann mein Leben,
> dort muss ich es lassen".

# DAS MITTELLAND

Der spanische Eroberer lässt sich zunächst an der Küste nieder, dort wo ihn seine Schiffe hinbringen. Von da ab muss er mit den Eingeborenen klarkommen, die ihn mal freundlich, mal feindselig empfangen. So treten der Übersetzer, der freundschaftlich gesinnte Indianer, das Geschäft, der Tausch, die Verständigung und die Konfrontation in Erscheinung.

Eine der ältesten Erzählungen über dieses Gebiet stammt aus dem Jahre 1532, geschrieben von Nicolás Federmann, Stellvertreter des Gouverneurs aus dem Hause der Welser, der über seine Expedition von Coro bis in die Tiefebenen auf der Suche des El Dorado und des Südmeeres, wie damals der Pazifik genannt wurde, ein Tagebuch führte. Besagtes Tagebuch beschäftigt sich wenig mit der Umgebung und konzentriert sich auf die Beschreibung der freundschaftlichen oder feindlichen Geschäfte, die die Expeditionsgruppe auf ihrer Reise mit den Indianerstämmen abschloss.

Die damaligen Geschichtschreiber Pedro Simón, Oviedo y Baños, sowie Alonso de Herrera, beschrieben die zentrale Region —das Mittelland— und die Mühseligkeit ihrer Kolonisierung. Davon zeugen die Gründungsdaten der diversen Städte: Barquisimeto 1552, Valencia 1555, Los Teques 1703, während Maracay erst 1743 den Stand als Gemeinde erhält.

Die Bundesstaaten Miranda, Aragua, Carabobo, Yaracuy und Lara bilden die Mitte des Landes, sowohl in historischem als auch in wirtschaftlichem und geographischem Sinne. Im Jahre 1567 wird die Hauptstadt der Provinz Venezuela von Coro nach Caracas verlegt. Von da ab führen alle Wege ins Mittelland, wie die Speichen eines Rades. Daher durchqueren unsere ersten Eisenbahnen auch das Mittelland, sei es nun die Strecke Valencia-Caracas, Puerto Cabello-Valencia, Caracas-La Guaira, Puerto Carenero-El Guapo oder Barquisimeto-Tucacas. Letztgenannte gilt als älteste Eisenbahnstrecke Südamerikas; alle Strecken wurden im 19. Jahrhundert gebaut.

Die Staaten des Mittellandes sind der wichtigste Schauplatz des Befreiungskrieges, wo die erste und die zweite Republik gewonnen und verloren wurde. Und abermals in diesem Gebiet festigt sich schliesslich die Unabhängigkeit des Landes. Alle grenzen ans Meer, mit Ausnahme der Staaten Yaracuy und Lara. Letztgenannter Bundesstaat wurde für die Zwecke dieser Erzählung an das Mittelland angeschlossen.

Der Bundesstaat Miranda wurde nach Francisco de Miranda benannt, der sein ganzes Leben der Befreiung nicht nur Venezuelas, sondern des südamerikanischen Kontinents gewidmet hat, "Vorbote" genannt wurde und die Nationalflagge entwarf. Der Bundesstaat Miranda umringt Caracas, dem er als Sauerstoffspender und Auslauf für die Hauptstadt dient, mit der er eng verschlungen ist. Diese Verknüpfung geht so weit, dass einige öffentliche Dienste gemeinschaftlich geleistet werden. In Miranda liegt Barlovento, "von wo der Wind herkommt", ein seit der Kolonie bestehendes Kakaoanbaugebiet, reich an Folklore und Bräuchen.

Die Küste des Bundesstaates Miranda erstreckt sich von Boca de Uchire bis Chuspa am zentralen Küstengebiet. An ihr liegt die schöne Tacarigua-Lagune, 30 km lang, die zum Nationalpark erklärt wurde. Mit einem Regenfall von über 1.000 mm im

Jahr und einer Temperatur zwischen 24 und 38 Grad Celsius, ist die Tacarigua-Lagune ein Reservoir für Halophyten —salzliebende Pflanzen— unter denen die rote Mangrove (Rhizofora mangle), die schwarze Mangrove (Avicennmia germinans) und die weisse Mangrove (Laguncularia racemosa) zu erwähnen wären. Ornithologen werden hier ihre besondere Freude haben, da in und um die Tacarigua-Lagune zahlreiche Vertreter der Gattungen der Ibisse (Threskiornitidae), Flamingos (Phoenicopteridae) und Möwen (Laridae) anzutreffen sind.

Im Bundesstaat Aragua wird hauptsächlich Landwirtschaft betrieben, obwohl seit 1960 auch Industriegebiete entstanden sind. Vom Naturschutzaspekt aus gesehen, beherbergt dieser Staat den ältesten Nationalpark Venezuelas, den im Jahre 1937 gegründeten "Rancho Grande"-Park, der später zu Ehren des Wissenschaftlers Henri Pittier, welcher zwischen 1930 und 1940 alle seine Anstrengungen der Erhaltung dieses Parks widmete, auf dessen Namen umgetauft wurde. Abgesehen von der vielfältigen Flora und Fauna kann man hier den höchsten Baum Venezuelas beobachten: den Cucharón oder Niño (Ghyrantera caribensis), der bis zu 50 Meter hoch wird.

Die Bundesstaaten Aragua, Carabobo und Yaracuy weisen sehr ähnliche geographische und klimatische Bedingungen auf. Es wird dort hauptsächlich Landwirtschaft und Leicht- bzw. mittelschwere Industrie betrieben, vornehmlich um die Städte Maracay und Valencia herum. Der Dichter und Schriftsteller Luis Pastori hat die Gegend wie folgt beschrieben: "Die alten Samanes dekorieren die Täler wie ehrwürdige Reliquien, an den Hängen der Hügel strahlt das kräftige Gelb der Araguaneyes; auf den Bergen leihen die blühenden Bucares ihr Scharlachrot den romantischen Beeren des Kaffestrauches, dem sie Schatten spenden".

Im Bundesstaat Lara gibt es ein bergiges, ein wüstenähnliches und ein flaches Gebiet. Grosse Flächen dienen dem Anbau von Sisal und Zuckerrohr, in einem Kampf der Halbwüste Land abzuringen. Überall erscheint und verschwindet der Mensch in Begleitung eines unzerstörbaren Vierbeiners, der sich scheinbar von allem —ausser von Steinen— ernährt: die Ziege. Rund um dieses Tier entstand ein ganzes Handwerks- und Ernährungssystem, dessen Erzeugnisse am Wegrand auf der Strasse von Barquisimeto nach Carora zum Verkauf angeboten werden. Barquisimeto wurde 1552 von Juan de Villegas gegründet. Der Name bedeutet aschfarbener Fluss.

Um Barquisimeto herum ist am Spätnachmittag eine ganz eigenartige Beleuchtung zu beobachten: ein Rot das zu Gelb wird und schliesslich in Blau übergeht. Es muss die Farbenpracht des barquisimetanischen Sonnenuntergangs gewesen sein, die den Komponisten Juan Ramón Barrios aus dem Staat Lara dazu inspirierte, die Lichtwellen in seinem Lied "Noches Larenses" im Ton festzuhalten:

Der Abend ist so schön,
alles ist still und ruhig,
unsere Seele ergötzt sich
am Licht der Sterne,
der unbefangene Mond
schleicht sich in den Garten
und streichelt die Rose
die der Brise Duft schenkt
und den Jasmin verschönert.

## DER WESTEN

Am 18. Mai 1499 stechen Alonso de Ojeda, Juan de La Cosa und Américo Vespucio vom Hafen Santa Catalina de Cádiz aus in See. Sie fahren die Orinoco-Mündung aufwärts, den Küsten der Paria und Araya-Halbinseln entlang und landen auf Margarita, setzen ihre Reise zu den Küsten von Macarapana fort und von dort aus zum Kap La Vela. Am 24. August gelangen sie an eine Lagune und "fanden überall in ihr, insbesonders an ihrem Ostufer, grosse Indianerdörfer vor, die an den Ufern und in den flacheren Teilen ins Wasser gebaut waren. Dort wo das Wasser bis an die Brust reichte, hatten sie ihre Häuser auf grossen Pfählen ins Wasser gesetzt und für alles Notwendige bedienten sie sich ihrer Kanus."

So erzählt es Bruder Pedro Simón in seiner zweiten Nachricht. Der Anblick erinnerte an Venedig und daher benannten sie diesen Ort Venezuela, Klein-Venedig, Namen den heute das ganze Land übernommen hat, dessen Westen durch die Bundesstaaten Falcón und Zulia gebildet wird.

Zulia ist eine Region mit sehr ausgeprägter Identität. Der unverwechselbare Sprachgebrauch, die Musik die durch die Gaita —heute die typische Weihnachtsmusik im ganzen Land— bekannt wurde und die Webkunst, bei der die Goajiro-Indianer ihre Tier- und Pflanzenphantasien in Farben umsetzen, die sie nie gesehen haben, sind alles Eigentümlichkeiten dieses Gebiets.

Der Bundesstaat Zulia liegt hufeisenförmig um den Maracaibo-See. Am Ostufer des Sees hat die Erdölindustrie einen Wald von metallischen Bohrtürmen gepflanzt. An der Westseite wird eine Vergangenheit erhalten, in der der Mensch noch heute in Pfahlbauten haust, vom Fischfang und vom Bootsbau lebt, wie seit der Zeit als der See noch der einzige Zugang des Gebietes- und Eingangstor der Anden war.

Die Maracaibo-Sandbank trennt den See vom Venezuela-Golf und stellt eine Art Unterwasserufer dar, das wenig Tiefgang für die Schiffahrt lässt und ständig ausgebaggert werden muss um die Durchfahrt zu ermöglichen.

Im Norden endet der Staat in der Goajira-Halbinsel, ein halb wüstenartiges Land das dem gehört, der es besetzt, mit Grenzen die die Einwohner nicht wahrhaben. Dort herrscht das Volk der Goajiro-Indianer, deren Dach der Himmel, Wände die Kakteen, Nachbarn die Familie und Familie der Stamm sind.

Die Stadt Maracaibo, Hauptstadt des Staates, wurde am 8. August 1529 von Ambrosio Alfinger gegründet, bei einer der wenigen Rastgelegenheiten, die er sich auf der unermüdlichen Suche nach dem "El Dorado", dieser mythologischen Stätte in der alles aus Gold ist, eingestand. Alfinger war ein Delegierter aus dem Hause der Welser, die für 18 Jahre "das Land zwischen dem Kap La Vela und dem Golf von Cariaco" zugesprochen bekamen, gemäss eines durch Karl V im Jahre 1528 unterzeichneten und im Jahre 1530 bestätigten Vertrages.

Bis 1962 lebte Maracaibo aufgrund seiner geographischen Lage relativ isoliert. Seitdem verbindet die Rafael Urdaneta-Brücke beide Ufer des Sees und die Stadt erhält somit Zugang zum Strassennetz das sie mit dem Rest des Landes verbindet. Die Stadt zeichnet sich durch ihre grossartige Vielfarbigkeit und ihre fröhliche Dynamik aus - so dass der Schriftsteller Rómulo Gallegos sie einst als "die Stadt, die niemals schläft" bezeichnete.

Der Bundesstaat Zulia ist mit ausgezeichnetem Boden ausgestattet, wo Landwirtschaft betrieben wird, und aus seinem Untergrund stammt mehr als die Hälfte der Erdölproduktion des Landes.

Wenn man nach Osten fährt gelangt man in den Bundesstaat Falcón, der in eine Bergkette und in die Wüsten oder Médanos (Wanderdünen) von Paraguaná und Coro aufgeteilt ist. Wenn die Wüsten vom ganzen amerikanischen Kontinent 3,5% ausmachen, so kann Venezuela froh sein, ihre eigenen in diesem Gebiet zu haben.

Paraguaná wurde von einem Dichter als "die Erben des Windes" genannt. Unbarmherzig und unaufhörlich bläst hier der Wind von Ost nach West. Es gibt kein Ausruhen, keine Pause, und die gesamte Vegetation bemüht sich ständig, sich aufrecht zu erhalten. Es verbleibt kaum noch Energie für den harten Ueberlebenskampf. Die Wolken ziehen vorbei ohne ihre wertvolle Fracht zu entladen, als ob sie dieses Land, das um einen Tropfen Feuchtigkeit zu flehen scheint, vollkommen ignorierten. Die Kakteen weiten ihre Arme aus auf der Suche nach dem Wasser, das sie sogar dem Morgentau abringen wollen. Das Wasser ist tatsächlich Leben.

Und in dieser Stille, die es gewohnt ist die Windböen zu verschlucken, scheint die Erde dazu verurteilt zu sein, fast wehrlos den Weg der Sonne zu beobachten: Sonnenaufgang, Zenith, Sonnenuntergang. Die Schatten beginnen mit dem schwachen Blau des Morgens um dann mittags zu verschwinden und schwarzbraun wieder länger zu werden, bevor sie ganz untertauchen. Die Sonne ist untergegangen und der Mond geht auf. Der Wind hört nicht auf. Und in dieser unerbittlichen Wiederholung des Gestern und Vorgestern öffnen sich die Kakteenblüten inmitten der rauhen Dornen. Es kommen die Bienen und die Vögel um den Nektar zu geniessen und um das Leben zu verteilen; es wird immer einen neuen Anfang und eine neue Gelegenheit geben.

Am Eingang zur Paraguaná-Halbinsel liegt Coro, die erste Hauptstadt Venezuelas, koloniales Heiligtum des Landes. Alles duftet nach Herkunft und nach Verehrung. Man atmet eine Luft herrschaftlicher Vergangenheit ein, in der es Zeit und Platz für alles gibt. Diese Atmosphäre muss den Schriftsteller Arturo Uslar Pietri inspiriert haben, folgende Zeilen zu schreiben, die an der Wand eines dieser Häuser von damals festgehalten wurden:

> "Der Wind und die Sonne erfüllen die engen Strassen von Coro. Ein schmaler Schattenstreifen fällt von den Dachtraufen auf den verbrannten Boden. Dicke Wände aus gestampfter Erde verteidigen die Häuser. Innen liegt ein Patio mit Bäumen und Blumen, umgeben von Arkadenfluren. In diesen tiefen Villen dicker Wände gibt es so etwas wie eine erhaltene und geklärte Frische, wo das Licht gesiebt und streichelnd eindringt."

# DIE LLANOS

"Yo nací en esta ribera del Arauca vibrador..." ("Ich bin an diesem Ufer des schwingenden Arauca geboren..."); so beginnt das Alma Llanera, Venezuelas zweite Nationalhymne. Nicht umsonst hat dieses Lied die Llanos, die Tiefebenen, zum Schauplatz, nehmen diese doch ein Drittel der Fläche des Landes ein und beherbergen ein Fünftel der Gesamtbevölkerung.

Die Tiefebenen grenzen im Norden an die Anden- und an die Küstenkordillere und im Süden an das Guayana-Massiv. Sie bilden die Becken der Flüsse Meta, Apure und Orinoco, als ob sie sich von Westen nach Osten ins Meer ergiessen würden.

Um dieses Tiefland, dessen Ursprung im Tertiär und Quartär liegt zu regionalisieren, wurde es traditionsgemäss in hohe und tiefe Llanos unterteilt, wobei die Grenzlinie um die 100 Meter über dem Meeresspiegel liegt. Heutzutage sind die Tiefebenen geopolitisch in die fünf Bundesstaaten Guárico, Apure, Portuguesa, Barinas und Cojedes aufgeteilt.

Diese Bundesstaaten bilden sowohl eine geographische, wie auch eine soziale, kulturelle und historische Einheit. Da es nichts gibt was sie trennt, gibt es vieles das sie bindet. Sie alle haben das Klima, die Vegetation, die Fauna und das Wesen ihrer Einwohner, der Llaneros, gemeinsam.

Seit der Ankunft Columbus' und der Eroberer aus Spanien wurden die Tiefebenen der kulturellen und religiösen Kolonisierung unterworfen, sowie der Rassenmischung. Zu den eingeborenen Indianern kommen die weissen Spanier und die schwarzen Sklaven hinzu.

Der Wissenschaftler und Entdeckungsreisende Alexander von Humboldt hält den sich ihm in dieser grenzenlosen Weite darbietenden Anblick in seiner Erzählung "Reise in die Äquinoctialgegenden des neuen Kontinents" wie folgt fest: Dieses grossartige Schauspiel des Sternenzeltes, in einer unermesslichen Weite dargeboten, die frische Brise die des Nachts durch die Ebene weht, die wogende Bewegung der Gräser dort wo die Ebene etwas an Höhe gewinnt, all' dies erinnerte uns an die Oberfläche des Ozeans.

Und in dieser Wahrnehmung scheint er alle Dimensionen, in denen sich die Natur zeigt, und auch den Menschen, den Llanero, als ob er ein Produkt dieser Natur sei, festzuhalten. Auf der einen Seite die Weite, das Fehlen jeglicher Grenzen, das Fehlen eines anderen Anhaltspunktes als den des tagtäglichen Weges der Sonne, und auf der anderen die Unbarmherzigkeit der Kontraste, Tag und Nacht, Ueberschwemmung und Dürre, Leben und Tod.

Die Umwelt ist durch die Beschaffung des Bodens, durch ihre Flora und Fauna, die Haustiere und die gezähmten Lebewesen, durch die Tätigkeit der Menschen, sei es um sich ihren Lebensunterhalt zu verdienen, um sich vor Sonne und Regen zu schützen, um sich mit anderen zu treffen, um als Gattung fortzubestehen oder nur um die Freizeit auszufüllen, gezeichnet. In einer Topographie deren Reliefs einzig und allein durch die Linie des Horizonts und das mit Wolken gesprenkelte Himmelszelt gegeben sind, ist die Natur bei der Ausstattung mit Pflanzen und Tieren verschwenderisch gewesen.

Die Flüsse schenken dem Menschen Leben in Form von Feuchtigkeit, Verkehrsweg und Nahrung, sie beherbergen aber auch furchterregende Feinde. So wie einerseits Fische wie der Pavón, der Coporo, der Valentón oder der Bagre den Speisezettel bereichern können, sind andererseits der Caribe, auch Piraña genannt, durch seinen zerreissenden Biss und der Zitteraal durch seine elektrischen Entladungen tödlich.

Der Chigüire, ein Wasserschwein, das grösste Nagetier der Welt, ist zeitweise in so grosser Anzahl vorhanden, dass es notwendig wird die Bestände zu dezimieren. Nicht so verhält es sich mit Rehen, den Pakas, den Tapiren und den Báquiros, kleinen Wildschweinen, die naturschutzbedürftig sind und für die Schonzeiten eingerichtet werden müssen.

In der Trockenzeit versammeln sich an den Ufern der Lagunen riesige Vogelscharen, die sich hauptsächlich aus Königsreihern, Schnabelreihern, roten und weissen Ibissen und Kormoranen zusammensetzen.

In den Llanos bekommt man den Eindruck, dass die Natur sich im ständigen Kampf zwischen dem Überfluss und der Knappheit befindet. Der Mensch hat versucht in dieses Ungleichgewicht einzudringen und der einem ungezähmten Fohlen ähnelnden Natur Zügel anzulegen. In der Nähe von Calabozo geschah es dann zum ersten Mal, dass man dem Wasser, das in gutem Masse so nützlich und im Übefluss so schädlich ist, die Freiheit geraubt hat in dem es aufgestaut wurde. So wird mit dem Überfluss aus der fetten Zeit die Not in der dürren Zeit gelindert - um ein so buchstäblich auf diese Situation übertragbares Gleichnis aus dem Alten Testament zu gebrauchen. Zu diesem Zweck wurden auch ähnliche Wasserstaumöglichkeiten im Bundesstaat Apure eingerichtet.

Da der Grund sandig und lehmig ist, können dort nur harte Gräser gedeihen. Ansonsten wird der Boden nur von kleinen Lagunen bedeckt, die sich in der Regenzeit bilden, unterbrochen von kleinen Sträuchern und Moriche-Hainen, eine Art Palme die sowohl Unterschlupf als auch Nahrung bietet.

Der Llanero, der Bewohner der Tiefebenen, verbringt sein ganzes Leben zwischen der Hängematte und seinem Pferd, letzteres gelegentlich für ein Kanu tauschend. Daher ist er im Wesen fast stoisch, ausserordentlich zäh und in allem was man auf oder vom Pferd aus erledigen kann sehr gewandt. Diese Eigenschaften kamen während des Befreiungs- und Unabhängigkeitskrieges zur Genüge zum Vorschein. Es waren die Llaneros, die Simón Bolívar auf dem Boyacá-Feldzug begleiteten, und sie waren es auch, die bei der Carabobo-Schlacht die Waagschale zugunsten der Patrioten neigten.

Der Llanero lindert seine Einsamkeit, indem er sich mit seinesgleichen trifft. Oft erscheint er in Begleitung von Wesen und Dingen, zu denen er eine Zuneigung verspürt: sein Pferd, sein Lasso, sein Kampfhahn, seine Harfe, das Cuatro —ein viersaitiges, gitarrenähnliches Instrument— und die Maracas. In diesen Momenten lässt er seinen Gefühlen freien Lauf, wobei er seine Weltanschauung preis gibt, die vielleicht am besten in folgender Strophe dargestellt werden kann:

Über den Llanos die Palme,
über der Palme der Himmel,
über meinem Pferd ich,
und über ich, mein Hut.

## DIE ANDEN

Von Feuerland und mehr als 9.000 Kilometer lang erstreckt sich die Andenkordillere nach oben, gleich der Wirbelsäule eines Riesen, über den südamerikanischen Kontinent. Bei einer Durchschnittshöhe von 4.000 Metern, bricht die Kordillere oft zu Gipfeln aus, deren Aufstieg der Wunschtraum eines jeden Bergsteigers ist, so wie der Aconcagua in Chile, der Huila und der Sierra Nevada in Kolumbien und der Bolívar in Venezuela, um nur jene zu erwähnen, welche die 5.000-Meter-Marke übersteigen.

Die Anden, deren Name höchstwahrscheinlich von den durch die Inkas in die Hänge gegrabenen Terassen (=andenes) stammt, erreichen Venezuela als Ostkordillere des Knoten von Pasto, um hier die Bundesstaaten Táchira, Mérida und Trujillo zu umfassen.

Seit über 15.000 Jahren von den Timoto-cuicas, den Aruacos, den Betoyes und den Caribes bewohnt, halten die venezolanischen Anden im 15. Jahrhundert ihren ersten Einzug in die geschriebene Geschichte, als Bruder Pedro Simón, Chronist der Eroberung, über die auf mit Steinmauern terrassiertem Boden angelegten Mais-, Baumwoll-, Ñame-, Sellerie-, Yucca- und Kartoffelfelder beeindruckt ist. Diesen Boden beschreibt Bruder Pedro Simón als schräg und unzugänglich.

Diese Unzugänglichkeit war sowohl für die Wirtschaft als auch für die Psyche des Andenmenschen bezeichnend. Die Andenbewohner gelten als diszipliniert und ausserordentlich arbeitsam. Bis 1925, als die transandinische Landstrasse gebaut wurde, fehlte es dem Gebiet voll und ganz an Verbindung von Ost nach West und alle Zufahrten liefen an der Südseite des Maracaibo-Sees zusammen. Um nach Caracas zu gelangen, fuhr man zunächst über den Maracaibo-See bis nach Maracaibo und von dort aus auf dem Seeweg, manchmal mit Zwischenhalt auf Aruba oder Curacao, weiter nach Caracas. Bis zu dem Moment, als drei Eisenbahnlinien gebaut wurden, die von Hafen Encontrados nach Táchira, die von Santa Bárbara nach El Vigía im Staat Mérida und die von La Ceiba nach Motatán im Staat Trujillo, alle Ende des 19. Jahrhunderts gelegt, wurde alles auf dem Rücken der Maultiere transportiert.

Den Lebensunterhalt des Gebiets bot die Landwirtschaft, hauptsächlich der Kaffeeanbau. Die auf dem Weltmarkt schwankenden Kaffeepreise sowie die Konkurrenz aus Brasilien hielten die Andenregion ständig in wirtschaftlichem Schach und oft ergaben sich Zeiten des Hungers und der Not.

Humboldt erinnert die Andenregion in seiner Botanikabhandlung Südamerikas wie "extrem rauhe Einsamkeit, der Unbarmherzigkeit der Stürme ausgesetzt, wo der aufgeweichte Schnee schmilzt; ein Gebiet das Tag und Nacht von den ungestümen Winden heimgesucht wird..." Diese Beschreibung kann nicht auf die venezolanischen Anden zutreffen. Man kommt in Begeisterung bei der Betrachtung der mit gelben Frailejones bedeckten Wiesen, die sich von glasklaren Flüsschen und Lagunen abheben, und schliesslich durch das kräftige Blau des unverschmutzten Himmels, das die weissen Gipfel umrahmt. Und es ist gerade dieser Frailejón aus edlem Samt, der in einer scheinbaren Opposition lebt. Im Gegensatz zum Rest der Pflanzenwelt wird er mit steigender Höhe über dem Meeresspiegel immer grösser.

Der landschaftliche Schatz dieses Gebiets wird durch den Nationalpark Simón Bolívar der Sierra Nevada bewacht, der 1952 geschaffen wurde, und umfasst den Bolívar-Gipfel, 5.007 Meter hoch, gefolgt von dem 4.942 Meter hohen Humboldt-Gipfel und dem 4.883 Meter hohen Bonpland-Gipfel. Auf dieser Höhe ist das Klima weit unter dem Gefrierpunkt. Weiter unten, bei ca. 3.600 Metern, beträgt die Temperatur rund 10 Grad Celsius. Von dort gelangt man in das sogenannte "kalte Land", in dem Wälder und Savannen vorherrschen und die Temperatur zwischen 15 und 9 Grad schwankt.

Die drei Bundesstaaten der venezolanischen Anden, Táchira, Mérida und Trujillo erfuhren in der Geschichte das Schicksal einer Art dreigliedriger Kette, deren Glieder an unterschiedliche Machtzentren gebunden waren. Während Trujillo ursprünglich zur Provinz Caracas gehörte, war Mérida —das damals noch Táchira mitumfasste— von Santa Fe de Bogotá abhängig. Erst durch die im Jahre 1777 von Karl III erlassene königliche Order werden die Provinzen Mérida, Nueva Andalucía und Guayana in die Statthalterschaft Venezuela integriert.

Die Andinos, die Leute aus den Anden, haben schon immer ein besonderes Verhältnis zur Macht gehabt, sei es die der spanischen Krone, die der Unabhängigkeitsbewegung oder die der Republik.

Bereits 1781 entsteht eine aufständische Bewegung die von den Regionalmachthabern unterjocht wird. Im Jahre 1810 schliessen sich die Andinos der Freiheitsbewegung an "um den Kopf zu heben und das Joch dieser Regierung, die uns bis jetzt unterdrückt hat, abzuschütteln". Als Vergeltung wurden das Kollegium, das Seminar und der Bischofssitz von Mérida nach Maracaibo verlegt. Und es ist gerade diese Stadt Mérida, die Simón Bolívar 1813 zum ersten Mal den Titel "Befreier" verleiht.

Die Andinos haben es nicht nur verstanden, gegen die Macht der Krone anzugehen, sondern auch die eigene Macht auszuüben, in dem sie Venezuela die Präsidenten für mehr als ein Drittel der Unabhängigkeitszeit stellten.

Heutzutage ist die wirtschaftliche Basis dieser traditionsgemäss landwirtschaftlich orientierten Region um die sogenannte Industrie ohne Schlote, den Tourismus, erweitert worden. Die wichtigste Touristenattraktion stellt die Seilbahn Mérida-Pico Espejo dar, die längste und höchste Seilbahn der Welt.

Jeder Winkel in den Anden ist in irgendeinem Ausdruck der Schönheit einzigartig. Um aber das Erhabene erleben zu können muss der Mensch wieder zu sich selbst kommen und die Ikarus-Flügel, die ihm die Transportmittel simulieren, abschütteln um dann einen der magischen Gipfel zu erklimmen, die als die fünf weissen Adler gelten:

der Bonpland
der Humboldt
der Bolívar
der Toro und
der León.

# EL ORIENTE

Anzoátegui, Monagas, Nueva Esparta y Sucre

A window in the El Caserio
Craft Museum. Island of Margarita.

Fenster des Handwerksmuseums,
El Caserío. Insel Margarita.

The sun rises over the El Agua
Beach on the Island of Margarita.

Tagesanbruch am Strand El Agua.
Insel Margarita.

Island of Margarita. Part of the 10.700 hectares of the Laguna de La Restinga National Park.

Insel Margarita. Lagune La Restinga, ein 10.700 Ha grosser Nationalpark.

Manzanillo Beach, Island of Margarita.
White sands, blue seas, green hills.

Playa Manzanillo: weisser Sandstrand und türkisfarbenes Wasser, von Hügeln eingerahmt. Insel Margarita.

Fishing boats on El Tirano
Beach. Island of Margarita.

Playa El Tirano:
Insel Margarita.

In the tropical sunset, »»»
Juan Griego bay displays a
variety of colors.

Die Bucht von Juan Griego in der »»»
vielfältigen Farbenpracht
einer tropischen Abenddämmerung.

A cannon on the Galera Fort
guards Juan Griego bay.

Die Kanone des Fort La Galera
wacht über die Bucht von Juan Griego.

The castle of San Antonio de la Eminencia
in Cumana. Its four pointed star shape
was finished in 1686.

Festung San Antonio de la Eminencia in Cumana,
im Jahre 1686 fertiggestellt, mit dem
Grundriss eines vierzackigen Sternes.

The Island of Silver,
state of Anzoategui.

Isla de Plata, im
Bundesstaat Anzoátegui.

Bathing in the sun,
bathing in the water.

Wasserbad - Sonnenbad.

A cheerful
and guileless smile.

Ein Lächeln voller
Offenherzigkeit und Optimismus.

Playa Colorada,
Sucre state.

Playa Colorada, im
Bundesstaat Sucre.

Endless waves, a seemingly endless beach.

A bird's eye view of an eastern beach. »»»

Die Wellen jagen sich ohne dass je eine die andere einholt.

Ein Strand im Oriente, aus der Vogelperspektive. »»»

Agriculture, crafts, fishery:
mainstays of eastern Venezuela.

Landwirtschaft, Handwerk und Fischfang:
Lebensunterhalt des Menschen im Osten.

The moon looks down
at the palm at
San Juan de las Galdonas.

Mond und Palme,
San Juan de las Galdonas.

Pelicans
crowd on a reef.

Pelikane über
einem Korallenriff.

Making use of the wind...



Im Wind...

...and the sun.

...und in der Sonne.

A giant pallette of colors
at the Araya salt works.

Die Araya-Salinen,
eine Farbenpalette.

Salt foam at Laguna Madre,
Araya peninsula.

Salzschaum an der Laguna Madre,
Araya-Halbinsel.

The ancient ritual of
cassava root preparation.



Bei der Zubereitung des Casabe.

A gathering of brightly
clad dolls graces
El Cerezal.

Puppentreffen
in El Cerezal.

# GUAYANA

Bolívar, Territorio Federal Amazonas y Territorio Federal Delta Amacuro

Canaima lake sums up the region: »»»
tepuyes, the rust-colored river, the jungle,
the skies and the clouds.

Um die Canaima-Lagune sind die Elemente der Region »»»
gesammelt: die Tepuyes, der rötlichbraun gefärbte Fluss,
die Pflanzenwelt, der Himmel und die Wolken.

Upriver, from Canaima
to Auyantepuy.

Von Canaima,
zum Auyantepuy.

White rocks, red rocks, red waters,
a dugout canoe, with tepuyes
brooding in the background.

Weisse Felsen, rote Felsen, rotes Wasser,
Curiara-Einbaum und Tepuyes.

The Carrao river requires
great river-craft.

Die Fahrt auf dem Carrao
erfordert viel Geschicklichkeit.

At last, Angel Falls in the distance, »»»
over 1,000 meters high.

Endlich ist er zu sehen, »»»
der majestätische Angel-Fall,
über 1.000 Meter hoch.

At the top of Roraima.
"The Lost World".

Auf dem Gipfel des Roraima.

In indian dialect Roraima means
"mother of the waters". Here it can be
seen next to the Kukenan tepui.

Der Roraima, in der Pemón-Sprache,
die grosse und immer fruchtbare Mutter der Flüsse,
mit dem Kukenán-Tepuy.

An Orinoco river ferry.



"Chalana" Fähre auf dem Orinoco.

Carnestolenda flower.

Jasper creek. »»»

Carnestolenda.

Quebrada de Jaspe, »»»
der Jaspis Wasserfall.

A tree becomes a boat:
the curiara or dugout canoe.

Die Curiara:
ein zu Boot gewordener Baum.

The evening sun colors »»»
the rapids and channels
of the Orinoco.

Der Orinoco mit seinen Stromschnellen, »»»
von der untergehenden Sonne
in Pastelltöne getaucht.

Plowing furrows in the infinite river.



Den unendlichen Fluss durchziehend.

In Delta Amacuro,
everything must move upon water.

Im Delta Amacuro
geht alles auf dem Wasser vor sich.

Indian children in their natural environment.

Indianerkinder in ihrer eigenen Welt.

A churuata under construction, built to be part of the forest itself. »»»

Eine Churuata im Bau: indianische Behausung die in der Landschaft untergeht. »»»

Rapids form a barrier
between ocean and jungle.

Die Stromschnellen sind Navigationshindernisse
zwischen Ozean und Urwald.

The Atures rapids divide
the upper and lower Orinoco.

A bongo, rigged out as a living quarter, »»»
surveys the sunset at Port Samariapo.

Die Atures-Stromschnellen: Trennlinie
zwischen oberem und unterem Orinoco.

Ein zur schwimmenden Behausung gewordener Bongo. »»»
Hafen von Samariapo.

# CARACAS

The freeway seems to be »»»
swallowed by the buildings.

Die Autobahn verliert sich »»»
zwischen den Hochhäusern.

HONDA

A new symbol of Caracas,
Parque Central.

Parque Central,
neues Wahrzeichen der Stadt.

The La Pastora district, with
its turn-of-the-century houses.

The Pulpo —octopus— interchange »»»
carpeted with lights at day's end.

Die Architektur der Jahrhundertwende blieb
in La Pastora erhalten.

Der Pulpo —der Polyp— wird in der »»»
Abenddämmerung in ein Lichtermeer getaucht.

HOTEL
HOTEL

Time spent with the children
is never enough.

Man kann den Kindern
nie genug Zeit widmen.

The children's museum has its
own unique color scheme.

Das Museum für Kinder
erfreut sich seiner eigenen Farben.

The Autopista del Este,
ribbons of concrete
spanning the valley.

Die Autobahn des Ostens,
ein Betongeflecht.

San Bernardino, one of the older
neighborhoods, at the foot of
the mountains.

San Bernardino,
einer der ältesten Stadtteile.

Conceived as a temporary solution,
now a permanent feature.
Ranchos or shacks.

Die Ranchos, ein sesshaft
gewordenes Provisorium.

There will always be fruit and
people to sell it, in Caracas.

Der Obsthändler fehlt nie
in den Strassen von Caracas.

During rush hour, streets
turn into parking lots.

The eastern part of the city. »»»

Zu mancher Stunde werden
die Strassen eher zu Parkplätzen.

Der Osten der Stadt. »»»

The Cathedral.

The Capitol, dating back to the last century. »»

Die Kathedrale.

Das Kapitol stammt aus dem vorigen Jahrhundert. »»

CONSTRUIDO BAJO LA ADMINISTRACION
DEL ILUSTRE AMERICANO
GENERAL ANTONIO GUZMAN BLANCO
1877

«««« The Teresa Carreño Theater, with sculpture by Jesus Soto on the ceilling.
«««« «««« The Santa Capilla church.

«««« Das durch eine Skulptur von Jesús Soto dekorierte Teresa-Carreño-Theater.
«««« «««« Santa Capilla.

The guard of honor, at the founding father's memorial Los Proceres.

Die Ehrengarde huldigt den Freiheitshelden.

Monuments mirrored in a reflecting pond,
in Los Proceres Avenue.

Wasser-Spiegel.
Avenida Los Próceres.

Simon Bolivar University,
formerly the Sartenejas Hacienda.

Die Simón Bolívar-Universität,
in der ehemaligen Hacienda Sartenejas gelegen.

Cramming for an exam
at the Universidad Central.

Vorbereitung auf eine Prüfung
in der Zentral-Universität.

A view of the Caracas subway,
at the Colegio de Ingenieros station.

U-Bahn-Station:
Colegio de Ingenieros.

The Caracas subway,
pride of the public services.

Plaza Venezuela. »»»

Die U-Bahn "Metro" von Caracas.
Stolz des öffentlichen Verkehrsdienstes.

GRUPO
FINANCIERO
BANCOMARA
Coca-Cola
La clave es
SOLIDEZ
El BANCO DE MARACAIBO
AHORRAR
ES MAS FACIL
EN
FONDO COMUN
MAS AGENCIAS CERCA DE USTED

Savoy
PFAFF
COPAN'83
AEROPOSTAL

Simon Bolivar's birthplace,
restored to its original conditions.

Das Geburtshaus von Simón Bolívar.

Bolivar, as he must have been »»»
many times during his life:
alone in the rain, at night.

Bolívar, so wie er wahrscheinlich »»»
oft in seinem Leben war:
allein in einer Regennacht.

# EL CENTRO

Aragua, Carabobo, Lara, Miranda y Yaracuy

On Corpus Christi day,
the Devils of Yare dance.
Miranda state. San Francisco de Yare.

A graceful trio in »»»
Zuata National Park.

Am Fronleichnamstag tanzen
die Teufel von Yare.

Vogel-Trio »»»
im Zuata-Nationalpark.

Clouds in the water, water in the sky.
Zuata National Park.

Die Wolken im Wasser und das Wasser
am Himmel. Zuata-Nationalpark.

Camatagua Damm, Aragua.

Der Camatagua-Stausee.

«««  Sugar cane spikes seem to pierce the sky.

Stately Royal Palms frame a road in the Santa Teresa Hacienda.

«««  Zuckerrohrähren.

Eine Reihe Chaguaramo-Palmen, Hacienda Santa Teresa.

Venezuela's national instrument,
the cuatro, getting its finishing touches.



Die letzten Handgriffe am Cuatro.

"The Rising Sun", sculpture by
Cruz Diez, at twilight in Barquisimeto.

Die Skulptur "Die aufgehende Sonne" des Bildhauers
Cruz Diez vor der in Barquisimeto
sprichwörtlichen Abenddämmerung.

At the monument dedicated to the battle of Carabobo, an honor guard in period uniforms.

Die Ehrengarde mit Uniform aus der damaligen Zeit.

The archway commemorating the battle. »»»

Ehrenmal der Schlacht von Carabobo. »»»

1821
1821

Fruits of all flavors,
Puerto Cabello.

Obst in jeder Geschmacksrichtung.
Puerto Cabello.

An artisan remembers the past
and carves in the present.

Das Handwerk beschäftigt sich mit
Gegenwart und Vergangenheit.

The street of the Lanceros in Puerto Cabello,
the most portrayed street in the country.

Die Los Lanceros Gasse in Puerto Cabello,
die meistgemalte in Venezuela.

Yolanda.

The Solano Fort stood guard over
Puerto Cabello since Colonial times.

Das Solano-Fort wachte zur Zeit der Kolonie
über Puerto Cabello.

At night, Lancer's street
recalls the past.

The El Palito refinery. »»»

Abends ruft die Los Lanceros Gasse
Erinnerungen an längst vergangene Zeiten hervor.

Raffinerie El Palito. »»»

««« Mist and vegetation in the
Henry Pittier National Park.

The Choroni river flows gracefully
under its bamboo canopy.

««« Der Urwald im Nebel.
Henri Pittier-Nationalpark.

Langsam windet sich der Choroní-Fluss
durch den Bambuswald.

Sunrise at Cuyagua.

Sonnenaufgang in Cuyagua.

Palms tree row Cuyagua.

Palmenarkade. Cuyagua.

Coconuts.



Kokosnüsse.

A sculpture, courtesy of
Cocus nucifera.

Skulptur einer Cocus nucifera.

Sun and shade,
Cata beach.

Sonne und Schatten
am Strand von Cata.

Cata Bay, as if it were
laid out by a compass.

First dip of the day, »»»
Cuyagua.

Die Bucht von Cata, als ob sie
mit einem Zirkel gezeichnet worden wäre.

Das erste Bad am Morgen, »»»
Cuyagua.

# EL OCCIDENTE

Falcón y Zulia

Morrocoy National Park,
a Caribbean pallette.

A palm tree grows, »»»
sheltered by its elders.

Im Morrocoy-Nationalpark sind alle
Farben der Karibik anzutreffen.

Langsam wächst die Palme »»»
im Schutze der Grossen.

Apamate in flower.

Mangle tree, »»»
Morrocoy National Park.

Blühender Apamate.

Mangroven. »»»
Morrocoy-Nationalpark.

Hueque Falls.

Der Hueque-Wasserfall.

Rebellion of colors.

Aufstand der Farben.

The house with the Iron Windows,
a symbol of Coro,
Venezuela's first capital...

Das Haus mit den eisernen Fenstern,
ein Wahrzeichen von Coro - der ersten
Hauptstadt Venezuelas...

...which preserves its
colonial architecture.

...in der die Kolonialarchitektur
noch erhalten bleibt.

Hammocks, hats, sandals,
and snacks. By the roadside,
everything is available.

Hängematten, Hüte, Alpargatas
und Nahrungsmittel:
alles kann man am Strassenrand kaufen.

Paraguana,
heirs to the wind.

Paraguaná,
die Erben des Windes.

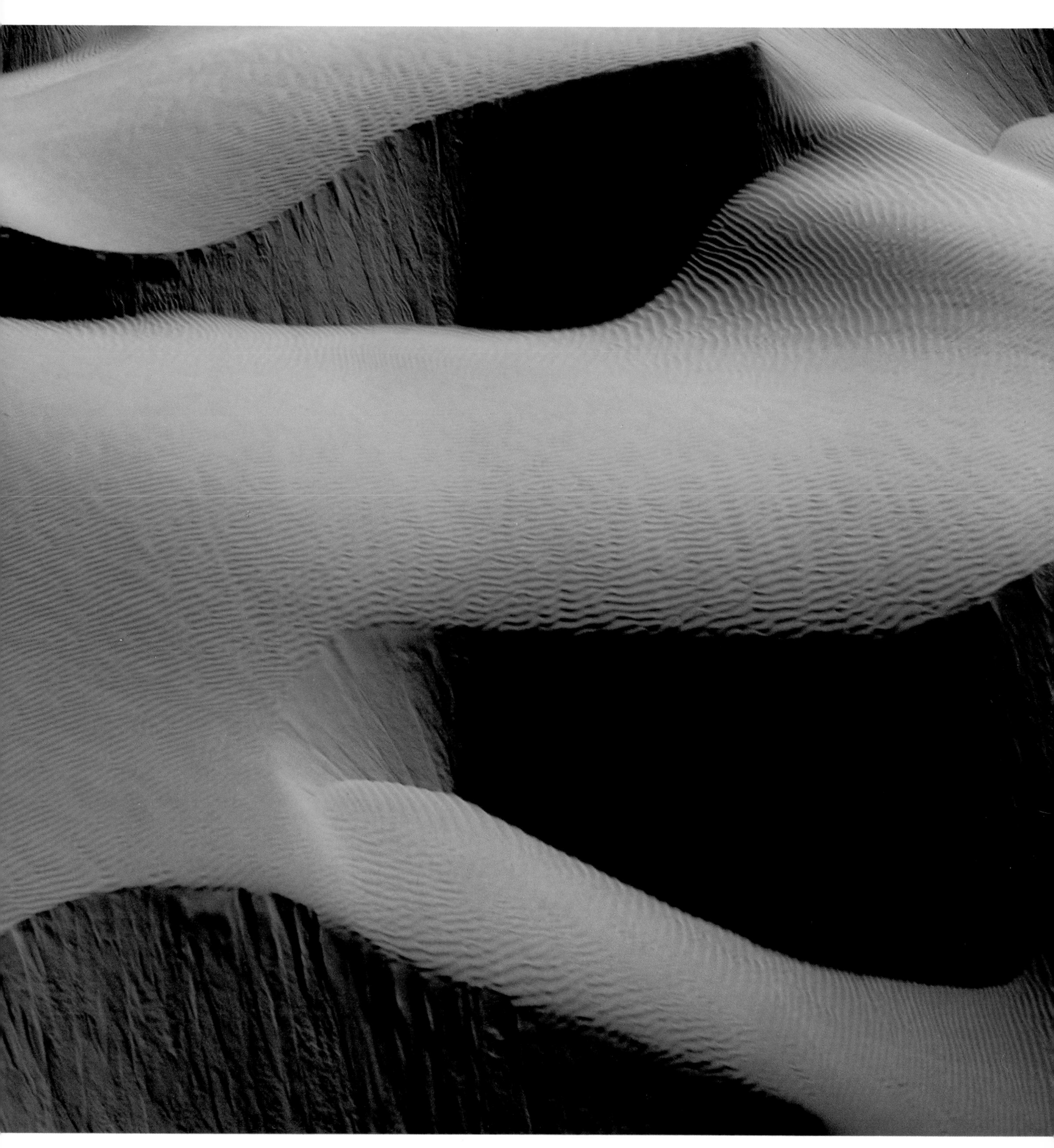

«««  Palm trees that refuse to yield.

The wind resculptures the sand every day.

«««  Unbesiegbare Palmen.

Jeden Tag gibt der Wind dem Sand neue Formen.

Home, halfway between
clouds and sky.

Mein Zuhause zwischen
den Wolken und dem Himmel.

The white bulk of the church
at Puerto Cumarebo
contrasts with the blue.

Die Kirche von Puerto Cumarebo,
eine weisse Tridimensionale
auf blauem Hintergrund.

Sunset at Punta Macolla. »»»

Abenddämmerung in Punta Macolla. »»»

Sinamaica.

Lights and shadows
in a lake hut at night.

Lichter und Schatten bemalen die
Palafito-Pfahlbauten in der Nacht.

The guajiro's colors are born
in his imagination,
not in his environment.

Der Guajiro-Indianer webt eine
Geschichte voller Farben die er selbst
noch nie gesehen hat.

Guajiro composition and art
poured onto a tapestry.

Die Aesthetik und Komposition der Guajiros
schlagen sich auf einem Wandteppich nieder.

This woman is as colorful
as her wares.

Die Frau als Teil
der Szenerie.

Houses and hues of Maracaibo.

The bridge over lake Maracaibo »»» in its evening finery.

Häuser und Farben in Maracaibo.

Am Spätnachmittag hüllt sich die Brücke »»» über den See in Licht.

# LOS LLANOS

Apure, Barinas, Cojedes, Guárico y Portuguesa

The Hills of San Juan de los Morros, »»»
guardians of the Llanos.

Die Morros de San Juan »»»
—die Felsen von San Juan—
wachen über die Llanos.

The llanero, hardy, hospitable,
and burnt by the sun.

Der Llanero, der Bewohner der Llanos,
derb und gastfreundlich, von der Sonne gegerbt.

Horses on the plain.

Pferde in der Ebene.

Life-giving sun,
life-destroying fire.

Die Sonne schenkt das Leben,
und das Feuer zerstört es.

Drought and flood
take turns in the Llanos.

Wasser und Dürre folgen
aufeinander in den Llanos.

A Moriche palm grove in the wet season,
Camaguan.

Moriche-Hain in der Regenzeit.
Camaguán.

Man, horse, and cattle,
always inseparable.

Mensch, Pferd und Vieh,
immer beisammen.

The Araguaney,
national tree of Venezuela.

Der Araguaney,
Nationalbaum Venezuelas.

Cranes, cattle, pasture and water.
A tableau in the El Frio Ranch.

A gathering of cranes. »»»

Reiher, Vieh, Gras und Wasser,
Hacienda El Frío.

Reiher-Reigen »»»

Birds in symmetry.
El Frio Ranch.

Vögel in Gleichgewicht.
Hacienda El Frío.

Llano alligators and turtles
bask in the sun. El Frio Ranch.

Babas —Krokodile— und
Schildkröten in der Sonne.
Hacienda El Frío.

A watering trough,
shaded by an Araguaney.

Man on horseback, »»»
master of the Llanos.

Tränke im Schatten
eines Araguaney.

Der Mann zu Pferde, »»»
Herr der Llanos.

The Chiguire, largest of the rodents.
El Frio Ranch.

Der Chigüire,
das grösste aller Nagetiere.
Hacienda El Frío.

Time to take shelter
as light slowly vanishes.

Das letzte Licht,
Zeit für die Nacht unterzukommen.

There is no road.
It will open up as you navigate.

Es gibt keinen Weg
er wird während der Fahrt gemacht.

Trees flooded
during the wet season.

Bäume in der Regenzeit.

Water in the gourd,
gourd attached to the waist.

Wasser in der Totuma
und die Totuma um die Hüfte.

Which one looks best?

Welcher steht mir besser?

There is no fair without a queen...

Kein Fest ohne Königin...

...nor a bullfight without aficionados.

...und kein Stierkampf ohne begeistertes Publikum.

Limitless pasture and cattle.

Sunset at Camaguan. »»»

Vieh und Weideland ohne Grenzen.

Sonnenuntergang in Camaguán. »»»

# LOS ANDES

Mérida, Táchira y Trujillo

Man and his work
blend into the landscape.

Der Mensch und sein Werk
in die Umgebung eingepasst.

The tilled top of the Esnujaque mesa.

Das bestellte Esnujaque-Plateau.

A yoke of oxen.

Ochsengespann.

A warm welcome at the gate.

Empfang am Tor.

Spinning tops, Piñango.

Kreiselspiel, Piñango.

Even the bees are fooled
by these lilies.

Blumen, die Lilien nachahmen
und sogar die Bienen täuschen.

There is a world of affection
in these dolls.

In diesen Puppen steckt eine
Welt der Zuneigung.

The town of Jaji, little changed
since colonial times.

In Jají hat sich seit
der Kolonialzeit wenig geändert.

Los Frailes,
a place to elevate the spirit.

Ein Ort um den Geist zu erheben:
Los Frailes.

Rest in peace.



Requiescat in pace.

Tilled fields.

Bestelltes Land.

In winter,
the frailejon is covered with snow...

In der Regenzeit wird
der Frailejón vom Schnee bedeckt...

...and at night
it turns into a monument.

...und in der Nacht
wird er zum Denkmal.

An andean house:
earth walls, tiled roof, and whitewash.

Das Haus in den Anden:
Ziegel, Erde und Kalk.

Children and Mucuchies pups.

The Laguna Negra »»»
changes hues as clouds roll by.

Beim Vorbeiziehen der Wolken ändern »»»
sich die Nuancen der Laguna Negra,
der schwarzen Lagune.

Kinder und Mucuchíes-Welpen.

The river winds
its way among mountains.

Der Fluss sucht sich seinen
Weg zwischen den Bergen.

Serene valleys and villages
on the Piñango road.

Täler und Orte die sich nicht
stören lassen, Strasse nach Piñango.

The El Carmen rustic chapel,
San Rafael of Mucuchies,
3,000 meters high.

Die kunsthandwerkliche Kapelle
in San Rafael de Mucuchíes,
in 3.000 Meter Höhe.

This child's face has picked up sun,
wind, and earth.

Im Gesicht des Kindes fangen sich Sonne,
Wind und Erde.

Merida and its cable car.



Mérida und seine Seilbahn.

Bolivar peak, over 5,000 meters
above the sea...

...adorned in summer »»»
by flowering bucare trees.

Der Bolívar-Gipfel ragt
über 5.000 Meter ü.M. hinaus...

...und im Sommer wird er von »»»
blühenden Bucare-Bäumen eingerahmt.

EDITORIAL AURORA C.A.
APARTADO 50916
CARACAS 1050A
VENEZUELA